What people are saying about

Astrology's Magical Nodes of the Moon

Astrology's Magical Nodes of the Moon was a real eye-opener. Although I consider myself a believer and follower of astrology, I have never had any astrologers explain the importance of the nodes of the Moon and how they connect us with our past life gifts, talents, and karma and help us pave the way toward our future and present life soul's purpose. This book is fantastic! I learned a lot about myself through the author's easy-to-follow compassionate guidance. Carmen Turner-Schott and Bernie Ashman have a real winner here. I highly recommend *Astrology's Magical Nodes of the Moon* to anyone who wants to understand their soul's purpose more deeply.

Shelley A. Kaehr, Ph.D., author of *The Goddess Discovered* and *Past Lives in Ancient Lands & Other Worlds*

T0019586

Astrology's Magical Nodes of the Moon

Releasing the Past & Embracing the Future

Carmen Turner Schott's Books

Moon Signs, Houses & Healing: Gain Emotional Strength &
Resilience Through Astrology
ISBN-100738773964

Sun Signs, Houses & Healing: Build Resilience & Transform
Your Life Through Astrology
ISBN-00738771309

The Mysteries of the Twelfth Astrological House: Fallen Angels
ISBN-101780993439

The Mysteries of the Eighth Astrological House: Phoenix
Rising
ISBN-109781450534505

Bernie Ashman's Books

Sun Sign Karma: Receiving Past Life Patterns with Astrology
ISBN-100738766917

How to Survive Mercury Retrograde: And Venus & Mars, Too
ISBN-100738745170

Sun Signs & Past Lives: Your Soul's Evolutionary Path
ISBN-100738721077

Astrology, Psychology, and Transformation
ISBN-101944662774

Astrology's Magical Nodes of the Moon

Releasing the Past & Embracing the Future

By Carmen Turner-Schott and Bernie Ashman

BOOKS

London, UK
Washington, DC, USA

CollectiveInk

First published by O-Books, 2024
O-Books is an imprint of Collective Ink Ltd.,
Unit 11, Shepperton House, 89 Shepperton Road, London, N1 3DF
office@collectiveinkbooks.com
www.collectiveinkbooks.com
www.o-books.com

For distributor details and how to order please visit the 'Ordering' section on our website.

Text copyright: Carmen Turner-Schott and Bernie Ashman 2023

ISBN: 978 1 80341 412 6
978 1 80341 413 3 (ebook)
Library of Congress Control Number: 2023938129

All rights reserved. Except for brief quotations in critical articles or reviews, no part of this book may be reproduced in any manner without prior written permission from the publishers.

The rights of Carmen Turner-Schott and Bernie Ashman as author have been asserted in accordance with the
Copyright, Designs and Patents Act 1988.

A CIP catalogue record for this book is available from the British Library.

Design: Lapiz Digital Services

Printed and bound by CPI Group (UK) Ltd, Croydon, CR0 4YY
Printed in North America by CPI GPS partners

The author of this book does not dispense medical advice or prescribe the use of any technique as a form of treatment for physical, emotional, or medical problems without the advice of a physician, either directly or indirectly. The intent of the author is only to offer information of a general nature to help you in your quest for emotional and spiritual well-being. In the event you use any of the information in this book for yourself, which is your constitutional right, the author and the publisher assume no responsibility for your actions.

We operate a distinctive and ethical publishing philosophy in all areas of our business, from our global network of authors to production and worldwide distribution.

Contents

Introduction

Have you ever been curious about your past lives? For many years, Carmen Turner-Schott and Bernie Ashman, the authors of *Astrology's Magical Nodes of the Moon*, have worked as astrological counselors with a strong interest in past lives. One of the main goals of this book is to introduce you to important past life themes that have accompanied you into this incarnation. Whether you are new to astrology or a professional, we believe you will find this book a helpful guide to navigate any past life shadows and achieve personal empowerment. The good news is that whatever might be working negatively for you can be turned into positive energy. This book will help you become more aware of past life patterns that could have become activated in this lifetime. This is the first step to channeling past life energy productively into your own creative pursuits and important life goals.

Part one of the book covers astrology's primary players: the planets, signs, and houses. We included this vital material to make reading and understanding part two on the nodes of the Moon easier. In the second section, you will discover your own personal past life history. The descriptions of the planets, signs, and houses can be used as a handy reference to keep in mind when reading about your past life themes. You may return to this first section of the book as needed when you read the interpretations of the nodes of the Moon.

Part two of the book introduces you to one of the most important facets in your astrological chart, the nodes of the Moon. The Moon's nodes in the birth chart show where your destiny lies and what past life themes need to be transformed. Astrologers look at the north and south node to dive deeply into what lessons an individual has to heal, let go of, and transform.

The sign and house of the south node of the Moon show what traits your soul already may have mastered with some karmic psychological patterns embedded in it. In Norse mythology, Loki represents the trickster and mischievous one. The south node is similar in influence and requires us to gain greater awareness when it becomes activated.

The sign and house of the north node are the personality traits we have to learn this lifetime. When we balance the north and south node, it attracts harmony, love, and creative success.

Understanding what sign and house the Moon's nodes are in keeps you clear about your main life priorities. The astrological north node sign and house are the areas of life we need to use productively in our daily lives. For instance, if the north node is in Taurus and in the second house, the person will learn how to find stability, safety, and security. They will need to focus on finding financial security and allow themselves to enjoy comfort. They will have to let go of a desire for constant change and upheaval. In past lives they may have experienced a lot of crisis, trauma, and unexpected transformations with the south node in the opposite sign Scorpio and in the eighth house. They are meant to master north node Taurus and second house energy and let go of stagnant Scorpio south node and eighth house energy. This is not to say the north node is better than the south node. Balancing these two forces produces positive expression.

This book offers tips on how to balance your own nodes of the Moon. Your north node and south node are always in opposite signs and houses in your astrology chart. Aligning this dynamic pair of nodes can feel like magic, and you experience harmony and abundance in your life. Past and present feel at peace, leading you forward to attain the love and success you hope to attain.

As the old saying goes, "Knowledge is power." In writing this book, we wanted to make your journey through each chapter go smoothly and provide you with greater clarity regarding challenges that might surface from past life patterns. The true value of this book is to give you the tools to transform the past life issues described into creative success and to point you toward paths of greater harmony.

The great Psychologist Carl Jung believed the universe regularly sends us synchronistic experiences, which he defined as meaningful coincidences. Astrology is both art and science. The art side of astrology represents the intuitive power each of us possesses to tune into new opportunities and to creatively paint the life that will bring us happiness inwardly and outwardly. In many ways astrology points to new doors being opened, allowing for new insights. The authors of this book believe each of us has freedom of choice. Hopefully the way the information is presented will awaken altered perceptions, allowing you to integrate past life patterns into a unique, new form of self-discovery.

Part One

Astrology's Main Characters—Planets, Signs, and Houses

What Are the Astrological Sun Signs, Elements, and Modalities?

There are twelve signs in the zodiac. Each one is ruled by a certain natural element: fire, air, earth, and water. Each sign is categorized by a certain modality: cardinal, fixed, or mutable. The modality of a sign is significant because it reveals a deeper part of the personality that others might not see. Each sign is ruled by a planet, and some signs share ruling planets. Mercury rules both Virgo and Gemini, and Libra and Taurus are both ruled by Venus. The fire signs (Aries, Leo, and Sagittarius) are full of energy and passion. The air signs (Gemini, Libra, and Aquarius) are intellectual and emotionally detached. The earth signs (Taurus, Virgo, and Capricorn) are practical and cautious. Cancer, Scorpio, and Pisces, the water signs, are emotional and imaginative.

The signs and planets have special symbols or glyphs associated with them. Aries, the Ram, starts the zodiac as the first sign and is ruled by the planet Mars. The second sign is Taurus, the Bull, which is ruled by the planet Venus. The third sign, Gemini, is ruled by Mercury and is known as the Twins. Cancer, the fourth sign, is ruled by the Moon, and its symbol is the Crab. Leo, the Lion, is the fifth sign and is ruled by the Sun. The sixth sign, Virgo, the Maiden, is ruled by the planet Mercury. Venus rules the seventh sign, Libra, which is represented as the metal scales of balance. Scorpio, the eighth sign, is associated with the Scorpion and the Eagle and is ruled by the planet Pluto. The ninth sign, Sagittarius, the Archer, is ruled by the planet Jupiter. Saturn rules Capricorn, the Goat, the tenth sign. Aquarius, the eleventh sign, known as the Water Bearer, pours out mental ideas quickly and is ruled by the planet Uranus. The final sign of the zodiac, the twelfth, is Pisces, the Fishes, which is ruled by Neptune. Below you can find your birth date, glyph, and Sun sign.

Your Sun sign is calculated by the month and day of your birth. An important note to remember is that if your birthdate is on the cusp, you might resonate with personality traits of both signs. For instance, if you were born on April 19, then you might have tendencies of both Aries and Taurus. Astrologers call this being born on the cusp, and sometimes the sign the Sun is moving into shows dominance and strength. However, there are exceptions as some individuals born late in a sign express more of the traits of this sign.

The Sun Sign Glyphs & Birth Dates

♈ Aries

March 21–April 19

♉ Taurus

April 20–May 20

♊ Gemini

May 21–June 21

♋ Cancer

June 22–July 22

Leo

July 23–August 22

 Virgo

August 23–September 22

Ω Libra

September 23–October 22

 Scorpio

October 21–November 22

✗ Sagittarius

November 22–December 21

♑ Capricorn

December 22–January 19

 Aquarius

January 20–February 18

♓ Pisces

February 19–March 20

Fire   Aries, Leo, Sagittarius   Masculine

Fire signs are known to be active, spontaneous, dynamic, and driven.

Air   Gemini, Libra, Aquarius   Masculine
Air signs are intellectual, aloof, detached, and inventive.

Earth   Taurus, Virgo, Capricorn   Feminine
Earth signs are practical, stable, determined, and hardworking.

Water   Cancer, Scorpio, Pisces   Feminine
Water signs are emotional, sensitive, compassionate, intuitive, and idealistic.

Polar Opposites

The most interesting fact about modalities and the easiest way to remember what signs are ruled by which quality is to look at what astrologers call polar opposites. The astrological wheel is made up of twelve houses, and each house is ruled by one of the twelve signs. Water and earth signs always oppose each other on the birth chart wheel, and fire and air signs oppose each other. No matter the day, time, or year, these signs are always across from each other in the sky. The most interesting thing is that polar opposites are always compatible elements and share the same modality—cardinal, fixed or mutable. There are four signs within each modality. If you look in nature, you can observe the elements at work. Fire signs are compatible with air signs. Earth signs are compatible with water signs. If you put water on fire, it puts the fire out. The same can be experienced when a fire sign and water sign are in a relationship. Fire stimulates action while water encourages us to pause and reflect. Air causes fire to grow in thought processes and to think of options, creating a compatible energy. The same can be seen with earth and water signs. Water helps the earth grow and blossom, and without the earth, water would have no home.

Polar opposite signs often get along well with each other unless they forget to compromise. These opposite signs have a natural way of understanding each other, which enhances compatibility. For instance, Aries will always oppose Libra, and their contrasting personalities actually complement each other. Polar opposite signs balance each other and bring out the best in each other. They also can challenge each other and bring greater awareness about their own weaknesses.

The following is an easy tip to remember the cardinal signs. These signs start the seasons of the year. Springtime arrives when the Sun is in Aries, and we see flowers blooming and new growth. Summer begins and the temperatures rise when the Sun enters Cancer. As fall approaches and the Sun travels into Libra, the leaves change colors and trees transform before our eyes. Then we have the winter season which is ruled by the sign Capricorn. During winter everything grows cold, and we hibernate and withdraw into our cocoon. Below you can see the modalities, the polar opposite signs, and the basic meanings.

Cardinal   Aries & Libra (Polar Opposites)
                Capricorn & Cancer (Polar Opposites)

Characteristics: Self-motivated, ambitious, activity starters, and enthusiastic about new ideas.

Fixed   Taurus & Scorpio (Polar Opposites)
                Leo & Aquarius (Polar Opposites)

Characteristics: Determined, strong-willed, stubborn, stable, purposeful, and absorbers of energy.

Mutable   Virgo & Pisces (Polar Opposites)
             Gemini & Sagittarius (Polar Opposites)

Characteristics: Changeable, easy-going, versatile, resourceful, and adaptable.

The Planets and Their Meanings

Traditionally there are ten planets we need to focus on when analyzing a birth chart: the Sun, the Moon, Mercury, Venus, Mars, Jupiter, Saturn, Uranus, Neptune, and Pluto. The energy of each planet is expressed more easily in some signs than in others. However, just as there are no good or bad signs, there are no good or bad planets. Each is a path to greater self-understanding. Each planet is associated with one of the twelve signs and is called a planetary ruler. A planet often feels totally at home and more flowing when it is in the sign it rules. An example is Mars placed in Aries, the sign it rules.

The term dignity in astrology refers to the strength or weakness of a planet in a sign. Some planets are easier for us to tune into when in a particular sign. This simply means that the energy expresses itself more easily or in a more challenging way when the planet is placed in that sign. The term exaltation means a planet may find easier expression in that sign. Venus, for example, is said to be exalted in the sign Pisces. The push to find a compatible partner that shares the same values and dreams can be part of having Venus in Pisces. Those with Venus in Pisces, however, need to stop trying to find a *perfect* person and keep expectations reasonable.

In the early days of astrology, planets were once said to be in their detriment when they were in the sign opposite of the one they rule. The Sun rules Leo, so the Sun was said to be its detriment in the opposite sign of Aquarius. This means the planet might have trouble expressing its energy and not feel comfortable placed in that sign. The authors of this book don't agree with this limited view. Too many exceptions to this viewpoint exist. The Sun in Aquarius, for example, possesses a powerful intellect. They can make great friends and allies and have numerous other attributes. Astrologers of the past also once thought a planet could be in its fall in a particular sign, meaning that the planet would have great difficulty expressing itself at all.

These planetary situations—exaltation, detriment, and fall—can each be channeled positively. Whatever sign houses one of your planets, its energy can become a valuable part of your soul growth and path to harmony and happiness! You are meant to evolve and find your own creative power through the planets placed in any sign.

The energy of each planet gives personality traits to that specific sign. This book will highlight each Sun sign's basic personality traits, the house associated with each sign, and the planets in those houses. Below is a cheat sheet to make it simple.

Image	Planet	Symbol Description	Glyph
Sun	Sun rules the sign Leo	The Sun represents your main identity, personality, and ego. The Sun symbolizes the father figure symbolically in your astrological chart. The house where the Sun is placed is where we like to shine.	Sun
Mercury	Mercury rules the signs Virgo and Gemini	Mercury represents your thoughts, ideas, and the way you communicate. The placement of Mercury is where you express yourself through writing and speaking.	Mercury
Venus	Venus rules the signs Taurus and Libra	Venus represents your love nature, beauty, and values. Venus symbolizes the way you express your love and feelings. Venus' placement is where you experience and seek harmony.	Venus

Image	Planet	Symbol Description	Glyph
Moon	Moon rules the sign Cancer	The Moon represents your emotional nature and inner life. How you express your feelings depends on which house and sign the Moon is in. The Moon represents the mother figure in your life.	Moon
Mars	Mars rules the signs Aries and Scorpio	Mars presents your drive, energy, aggression, and impulses. Where Mars is placed, you strive to succeed and are competitive. It can also show where you experience conflict in your life.	Mars
Jupiter	Jupiter rules the sign Sagittarius	Jupiter represents your life philosophy, abundance, education, and travel. Jupiter shows where you benefit and experience good luck and fortune.	Jupiter
Saturn	Saturn rules the sign Capricorn	Saturn represents where you feel discipline, leadership, responsibility, and where you might feel restricted. You are ambitious where Saturn is placed in your chart. Saturn stimulates career drive. Striving hard to reach goals is a Saturn influence.	Saturn
Uranus	Uranus rules the sign Aquarius	Uranus represents your individuality, uniqueness, and the ways you can be unusual. Anything unorthodox is Uranus energy. Uranus can represent sudden changes and the unexpected.	Uranus
Neptune	Neptune rules the sign Pisces	Neptune represents your highest beliefs, dreams, romanticism, and intuition. Neptune reveals where you find your spirituality and where you can delude yourself. It is associated with escape from reality. Believing in your highest goals can be linked to Neptune.	Neptune
Pluto	Pluto rules the sign Scorpio	Pluto represents emotional intensity, transformation, and regeneration. Pluto is where you experience empowerment and psychological changes within yourself. Pluto is passionate energy that is associated with sex, death, and other people's resources. A sense of renewal can manifest through Pluto.	Pluto

The Twelve Houses

The twelve houses in the astrological birth chart represent significant areas of life. The first house rules your main personality, appearance, and identity. The first house is known as the Ascendant or Rising Sign and is how others perceive you when they first meet you. The second house centers around money and finances. The third house is the house of communication, siblings, and basic learning. The fourth house deals with home and family. The fifth house is the house of children, creativity, pleasure, and fun. The sixth house is the house of work, routine, and health. The seventh house is known as the Descendant and rules marriage and partnership. The eighth house represents personal empowerment, forming trusted partnerships, healing, rebirth, trauma, and deep psychological experiences. The ninth is the house of foreigners, travel, higher education, and religion. The tenth house of career is also known as the Midheaven because it sits at the top of the birth chart wheel. The eleventh house governs friendship, individuality, goals, groups, and humanitarian causes. The twelfth house is the house of your higher beliefs, romantic feelings, intuition, sacrifice, spirituality, escapism, and service to others.

The powerful energy of your personality is expressed through these areas of life based on which planets are placed in each house in your birth chart. The planets have a certain energy, and where they land in your birth chart shows how this energy will affect that specific area of life. For example, if you were born late October, you will have the Sun in Scorpio. Someone born in the sign of the Scorpion is here to learn how to heal, transform, dive deeply into life, develop intimacy, and learn to trust others. The house position of your Scorpio Sun reveals where these lessons will occur. If the Sun is in the second house, then you will be learning to trust others with finances, build lasting security, and develop stability and to accept change on your own terms. Having a healthy self-esteem is of great value. When you know the meaning of each planet and then look at which house it's in, you can see where that energy will express in your life.

In certain chapters, we will describe people who have planets in a house as "a first house person" or an "eighth house person," which simply means that someone has planets placed in a certain house in their birth chart. When someone has more than three planets placed in one sign or house, we call this a stellium.

Many people ask why some houses are empty, and it's important to remember that it is perfectly fine not to have planets in certain houses. This simply means that when you were born the planets were not in that area of the sky. It does not take away from the importance of this house meaning in your life. The houses are represented by sections of the sky. The Earth sits in the middle of the wheel. If you imagine standing inside that wheel and looking up at the sky, it is divided into twelve sections, which are what astrologers call the houses or areas of life.

When we talk about a house cusp, we are referring to the specific sign that falls on that house on the birth chart wheel. For instance, if Virgo is your Ascendant, that sign might fall on the twelfth and first house cusp. If the Sun was placed on the cusp of the twelfth and first house, the energy of both houses can impact your life. If your birth date falls on the cutoff between two different signs, then you will want to read the personality traits of both signs to see which sign you resonate with the most.

Below we will briefly discuss each house of the birth chart and which sign is associated with it and explain the traits, life issues, and situations that each house represents.

First House: Aries

The fiery first house or Ascendant starts the birth chart wheel and represents the mask we wear in the world. Whichever sign falls on the first house cusp when you were born will show which type of personality you express to others. This energy is actually a mask or persona that hides your true inner nature. The ascendant or rising sign can display part of your identity that is different from your Sun sign. Others may observe you a certain way and sometimes they will misjudge you based on this. If Leo is on the first house, other people in the environment will often perceive you as attractive, magnetic, composed, and confident with an air of royalty when you walk into the room. When Leo is on the first house cusp, people in the environment often feel intimidated and perceive the person as self-assured.

The first house fully embodies all issues related to physical appearance. This is the house of the self and relates to issues such as ego, self-focus, health concerns, and tastes in dress. It is no surprise that fiery Aries naturally rules the first house, which is why the powerful energy of this house causes you to want to express the personality strongly, boldly, and in a straightforward way.

Individuals with first house planets might have difficulty holding back what they think and feel from others. They might enjoy acting aggressively at times, and taking risks excites them. The first house rules a person's overall behaviors, mannerisms, and drives. Having more than one planet in the first house often creates a personality that is intense, passionate, and extremely magnetic to others.

Second House: Taurus

As human beings we enjoy security and are not always comfortable with change. We like to plan for our future and set goals for ourselves. Many of us enjoy having money and believe that financial success will somehow make everything right in our lives. The second house of the birth chart relates to money, finances, security, comfort, and self-worth. It represents what we truly value in life both monetarily and emotionally. Your karma with finances, property, and comfort are associated with the second house. Your relationship with money depends on which planets reside in the second house. If Jupiter is in this house, for example, you may be the type of person who attracts money easily. If your financial karma is challenging, you might have Saturn in the second house, which can leave you feeling like you never have enough to feel secure, although working hard to achieve success is possible as well. This house shows our path to financial success and the creative ways we can make money and accumulate possessions.

It is no surprise that the earthy sign Taurus rules this house as most Taureans do not enjoy change and resist letting go of things. A major second house issue involves having difficulty relinquishing possessions, the past, emotions, and people. The second house reflects how you feel about yourself and who you are as a person. Learning to value yourself and the things that money cannot buy can be an important lesson of this house.

Third House: Gemini

As human beings we thrive by communicating with each other. Without communication and social interaction with others, we can become depressed and withdrawn. The airy third house plays an important role in how we think and express ourselves. The ability to communicate to others in all forms—through the written word, verbally, technologically through computers and telephone—falls under the third house. The third house is ruled by Gemini, the communicator and educator of the zodiac. Taking short trips and traveling from place to place are third house territory. Those with planets in the third house are usually intelligent and, depending on the planet, may have an increased ability to remember and recall information.

The spreading of information by whatever means available encompasses the third house's mission. Most planets in the third house will enhance your communication abilities and bless you with a gift of debate. Planets in the third house foster a need for constant mental stimulation and brain growth. Sometimes a break from too much outside input recharges the mental and physical energies. Nervous impulses that can manifest through the third house need to be productively channeled. The energy of this house is crucial for us to express ourselves in relationships with others. Learning to listen is a healthy way to use this landscape. The key is finding the right balance and allowing the creative energy of the third house to transform your life when you need it to. Then you can be rewarded with fresh perceptions and filled with renewed insights.

Fourth House: Cancer

Many of us remember the house we grew up in and all the neighborhood friends we had when we were younger. We might reminisce about the times we played sports with friends and siblings. You may easily recall your first crush in high school. Our most prominent memories relate to the type of childhood we had and especially to our parents and life inside our home. The watery fourth house symbolizes all the issues connected to our past, our childhood, our parents, and our roots. This house cusp is called the Imum Coeli, which is located at the bottom of the birth chart. The planets that reside in the fourth house reveal a lot about your relationship with your mother and issues you might have with nurturing. Becoming emotionally close with others is part of the fourth house territory.

The fourth house is one of the most important houses psychologically for us to adapt and grow as healthy individuals. As children we need a safe, secure, comfortable, reliable, and stable home environment to thrive within. If our home life and surroundings change or are unpredictable, it can impact us well into our adult years. If the change was for the better, we retain fond memories that strengthen us. The important lesson of the fourth house is for us to find our true home. We have the willpower and freedom to transform our future and make our current home life as comfortable and happy as we can imagine. Cancer rules the fourth house. This sign represents mothering and nurturing energy and is connected to caretaking, cooking, childcare, and a tendency towards needing privacy. A person may be able to intuitively tune in to any planet placed in the fourth house.

An individual with the Sun in the fourth house might have a strong desire to enjoy spending time at home. They may prefer to work from home. Some may feel perfectly content being a stay-at-home parent for their children. The fourth house pushes us to withdraw, hibernate, and isolate ourselves from the stresses of everyday life. It motivates us to create a home base to work from and a safe place to rest our troubles when life outside gets tough. Making peace with the past is sometimes linked to the fourth house. The universe sometimes drives us to move through fourth house energy and step out of our comfort zones to walk forward into the future to embrace new opportunities. This landscape can find us wanting to spend quality time with family, pets, plants, and our closest people.

Fifth House: Leo

The fifth house invites us to seek adventure and be open to new experiences in a big way. It is falling in love with life through creative imagination. Hobbies can become businesses. Childlike thoughts spring from this territory. When you love your everyday choices, it keeps your mind young.

Imagine becoming a parent and being responsible for raising a child. You can feel the excitement of watching a baby grow. In some ways this is the heartbeat of the fifth house, encouraging us to follow our most heartfelt dreams. Your mind may imagine winning an Olympic medal or making the winning three-point shot to win the game for your team at the buzzer. The house of pleasure, love affairs, excitement, sports, and pleasure sounds like an intriguing area of life. The fifth house is associated with children and any issues related to being childlike. This fiery house is one of the happiest places in the birth chart and brings a lightness of energy with it into our everyday lives. It is hard to find anything troubling about the fifth house because it is all about having fun and enjoying life.

The fifth house can show our interest and ability to be a parent or work with children in some way. We display this side of us when we act as a natural cheerleader for those we care about. We attract admiration and support from others by believing in them.

The energy of this house reveals our creative side and our drive for self-expression. Leo, the entertainer, rules this house, and it is no wonder that this life arena shows artistic talents such as music, writing, acting, athletic abilities as well as dancing talents. Fifth house planets often find their way into our work in the world. Some business people express the fifth house with great confidence in a charismatic way. The fifth house can display where we shine out in the world and what type of talents we have to embrace. Fifth house blessings include enjoying life, letting ourselves laugh, and finding joy as we hold our newborn baby for the first time.

A person sometimes can demand too much attention if their use of fifth house energy goes in the wrong direction. Sharing center stage is a better way to use the fifth house to keep a happy atmosphere in relationships.

Sixth House: Virgo

This is the house that rules health, diet, exercise, and maintaining mental strength. Having a healthy physical body and a positive attitude is important. Buddha is credited with saying, "Be vigilant; guard your mind against negative thoughts."

A stable, predictable, and healthy (versus toxic) work environment is vital to overall wellbeing. An unstable or unhappy work situation can truly affect us psychologically, mentally, and physically. The sixth house teaches us to stay grounded by having a routine. How we serve others in a practical way is sixth house territory. The universe tries to guide us to understand and embrace give and take in our relationships.

Some individuals can thrive in an unstable work environment better than others. The earthy sixth house is a place of structure, routine, hard work, and healthy diet. What we eat and put into our bodies, how much we exercise, when and how we relieve stress are all sixth house issues. The sixth house is known for perfectionism, worry, hypochondriac tendencies, and for being health conscious. The kind of work environment we thrive in and the type of relationships we have with co-workers relate to the sixth house.

Looking at specific planet placements in the sixth house can give insight about health and what types of diseases you might be vulnerable to. For instance, if Pluto is in the sixth house, often vulnerability in the reproductive region and elimination system may show up. Conditions like ovarian cysts, endometriosis, irritable bowel syndrome, and stress-related illnesses can manifest in the physical body. The energy of the sixth house affects our health even if we do not have specific planets placed there. Look at what sign is on the sixth house cusp to further investigate this. Many individuals with sixth house planets find themselves working in the medical field, in alternative healing professions such as energy work, acupuncture, herbal remedies, or in a hospital or clinical setting where they take care of others. People often work in service industries of various types through this earthy house.

Sixth house energy can manifest as obsessive-compulsive tendencies that can be traced to striving for too much perfection. For instance, someone with the Sun in the sixth house might feel uneasy or uncomfortable if they have not cleaned the dishes. They can't relax until the dishes are done. The important thing to remember is that this house has an influence on our daily lives and physical health. A good mantra for the sixth house is think positively.

Seventh House: Libra

This house is the gateway to enjoying intimacy and having romantic relationships with others. This people-oriented terrain may involve having business partners as well. Soulmate happiness is part of the seventh house package. Companionship can offer great joy and benefits in our lives. The airy seventh house is associated with marriage and our close peers as well as all the people we enjoy keeping close in our heart. Not only does the seventh house represent intimate relationships in our lives, it also reveals how we are in relationships and even what types of people we prefer as friends and lovers. Libra naturally rules the seventh house, the section of the birth chart that is referred to as the descendent. The sign Libra and seventh house energy focus on having companionship, and, as often as not, those with strong Libra choose to be without a close partner.

Certain planets that fall in the seventh house can have a significant impact on relationship development, partner choices, and relationship satisfaction. It is crucial to look at the seventh house in your own birth chart to determine which type of partner suits you best. Some individuals can relate to a wide circle of people. The sign on the cusp of the seventh house reveals the type of personality traits that may attract you and even how you might interact with someone in a relationship. A person with the Moon in the seventh house often feels empty without a partner. Some individuals experience anxiety whenever alone and need to have a relationship to feel fulfilled. Emotional security can be connected to having someone to love. Balancing dependency needs in relationships is key.

Certain planet placements in the seventh house can show positive developments in business partnerships. Some planets in the seventh house influence us to be cautious when trusting others. For instance, someone with the planet Uranus in the seventh house would be advised not to partner too quickly with others in business because of unexpected, unforeseen changes and their tendency to attract unreliable partners. As for marriage, waiting and truly getting to know someone before marriage would serve these individuals well because this placement can attract unpredictable or unstable intimate partners.

We can more closely understand the type of marriage we will have by looking at the seventh house. If there are not specific planets placed in your seventh house, then you will want to look at the sign on the seventh house cusp to determine the energy in your relationships and what might work well in maintaining closeness and trust in a relationship. Having someone to spend time with is important for our psychological wellbeing. We need others around us to cuddle, depend on, and communicate with. The seventh house is an important area of life where we can allow others to see our true nature and open up about things we might not readily share with others. If we are lucky, we may find true happiness with the perfect partner that encourages us, motivates us, and stands by us.

The Eighth House: Scorpio

The eighth house uplifts our self-confidence when we adapt to its intensity. Personal empowerment and getting a good sense of how to handle yourself in the world are linked to this passionate landscape. Our ability to form a profound bond with a parent, sibling, child, friend, or lover can be traced back to this deep, watery terrain. You have nothing to fear here even though it can test your mental and psychological strength during a crisis.

At some time in life, each of us deals with loss. Sometimes this can be the loss of a family member. Even the death of a pet can be difficult.

The eighth house does not always mean physical loss. Have you ever felt mentally lighter when working through a psychological problem? The hardest thing in life can be when the universe is trying to get us to surrender our negative thinking. We can get into a tug-of-war struggle as the universe tries to lighten our load. When we realize negative impulses must be let go, it can feel life a rebirth! This is the miracle of the eighth house energy.

Some of us are shielded from the death of others during childhood. There are people who experience death of someone close tragically at a young age. Losing someone we love through death is hard to understand, and many people do not even know how to talk about it. This house points out the taboos of society, the subjects that are hidden. All uncomfortable topics fall within the confines of the eight house in our birth chart.

Many subjects are hard to discuss. Some couples find it difficult to talk about money and what each would prefer to buy. Sometimes it is challenging to discuss sex openly. Maybe you want to tell someone their behavior is too critical but can't find the right words to verbalize your anger. Eighth house themes include issues such as abuse, trauma, rebirth, and sexuality, mystical topics, inheritances, other people's resources, family secrets, and the need to heal old wounds. The eighth house presents us with opportunities to learn regarding those things we find difficult to discuss because of their intensity or our own discomfort, such as child abuse, sexual assault, murder, death of our most cherished loved ones, and unexplained phenomena like ghosts. It is no wonder that the sign Scorpio is the natural ruler of the eighth house. Scorpio beats to the same drum of psychological depth as the eighth house. When thinking about the eighth house, the first thing that comes to my mind is the word "energy" — the subtle energy that surrounds our physical bodies, known as chi or prana, and how this life force can be used to heal others as well as ourselves.

When you have planets in the eighth house of your birth chart, you can be more sensitive to energy and subtle body language and can feel other people's pain and emotions. You may even pick up on their thoughts. Eighth house people see clearly through others with a laser-like intensity and with brutal honesty. What others show on the outside is insignificant because eighth house people will zone into their internal motivations, thoughts, deeper truths, and emotions. Bonding with others sexually and experiencing profound intimacy is an eighth house trait. A deep feeling of loneliness can be associated with eighth house planets. It is not unusual with eighth house planets to feel different from other people. You are sensitive, often intuitive, and have spiritual awakenings you can't explain.

Endings and beginnings of cycles are associated with the eighth house. When there are planets in the eighth house, death of a close family member or a friend often occurs at an early age. The eighth house makes us aware that people die and things change and allows us to recognize our own mortality. Many times with planets here, you inherit money, property, land, or spiritual gifts. The energy of the eighth house will create unexplained psychic experiences that usually start in childhood.

Eighth house people are born with natural intuitive abilities that might take time to tune into. Sensing the future and its opportunities can be a reality as well. Some eighth house individuals have a talent for knowing what others are thinking and feeling. This requires being aware of your boundaries. The true lesson of this house is to realize that transformation, rebirth, and change will make you more resilient. Healing others and allowing others to heal you are eighth house lessons. Many people with eighth house planets develop sharp business skills. Managing money is a skill. Management ability is one of the eighth house gifts.

The Ninth House: Sagittarius

Being born with faith and a strong belief in something greater than ourselves is a true blessing. We have the ninth house to thank for this gift. The ninth house rules all issues related to religion, philosophy, beliefs, law, history, and higher education. The ninth house awakens our desire to learn and study new subjects of interest. Our inner spirit of adventure emanates from this territory. This fiery house stimulates a desire to travel on the mental and physical levels. Traveling to foreign countries and visiting exotic places is part of this ninth house landscape. If you have planets in your astrology chart located here, you may travel far from where you were born or live in a different country. The ninth house is naturally affiliated with the sign Sagittarius, known as the wanderer, traveler, philosopher, and optimist. Ninth house energy is positive. It energizes and expands our awareness of the world around us. Those of us with planets in the ninth house may desire to achieve honors in education and obtain degrees in subjects that are important to us. For example, those with the Sun in the ninth house might find themselves joining the military or a volunteer foreign service. This puts them in touch with people who might speak a different language or have differing cultural values, which allows a ninth house person to view life from a dissimilar perspective. The energy of this house encourages diversity and an interest in different cultures.

The ninth house encourages movement and expansion. Those with planets placed here experience a restless desire to keep exploring new adventures. This can manifest as a great desire to travel, eat, and cook foreign food, or as falling in love with someone who was raised in another country.

I (Carmen) had a client who was single and had difficulty finding a marriage partner. I took a look at her chart and realized that she had the planet Venus in her ninth house. I asked her if she ever dated anyone raised in a different culture or background or someone who spoke a foreign language.

She looked at me and said, "No, I never thought about it."

With her Venus in the ninth house, she could find love while traveling or pursuing knowledge in another country. About two weeks after our discussion, my client called me. She started laughing and told me she met a man who was traveling to the United States from Australia. She wanted to let me know it was because she finally opened her mind up to meeting someone different and paying attention to where people were from. With ninth house energy, staying open to new ideas makes life more enjoyable.

No matter how hard life becomes, a sense of hope, understanding, and faith always resonates from the ninth house. Even in the midst of disaster or the depths of depression, individuals with ninth house planets will pick themselves up and try to be optimistic and practice gratitude. Something else interesting about the ninth house is that it can show our unique ability to be an influencer, counselor, life coach, and a great role model for others to not fear change. The gifts of the ninth house include faith, hope, and optimism in the face of adversity. Learning to embrace our unique beliefs and differences is something that takes great courage, and the ninth house can help us do that.

The Tenth House: Capricorn

Have you ever had the lines in your hand read by a palm reader? Think of the tenth house as your career and work line. Part of living in the practical world is working and earning money. Sometimes we get lucky and end up in a field we enjoy. At other times we just take the best job we can get. The tenth house shows which type of career fields we could be drawn to. The energy of this house can reveal how people see us in our public life and how we find success and get recognized for our talents. This earthy house involves personal drive, hard work, ambition, productivity, public image, advancement, and even politics. Tenth house energy can manifest by helping you make money and finding practical solutions to problems. The tenth house encourages us to work hard and remain focused to reach our potential. The rise to the top can be effortless when we channel the energy of planets placed here in a positive way. But the view can be lonely once they get there. Success does not always equal happiness. It is important to keep your friends and family close to maintain a sense of balance. Attempting to create win-win outcomes is a wise policy.

The achiever of the zodiac, the sign Capricorn naturally rules the tenth house. The energy of this house allows us to be patient and climb up the mountain just like the mountain goat. Starting at the bottom in a job position making minimum wage could just be the opening to greater success. This is the house of delayed gratification. The tenth house teaches us to do a job consistently and thoroughly.

With planets in the tenth house, we may feel drawn to a job in public service, government, politics, or real estate. The tenth house shows the way to be self-employed. We may have a strong desire to make money and be seen as successful in the eyes of others. Self-esteem is often connected to career success with planets in this territory. The tenth house is about being in the public eye. If the Sun is placed here, self-confidence in business usually radiates from the core. Dealing with the public comes easily as does achieving career goals. Idealistic Neptune in the tenth house can bring some uncertainty with career choices, requiring patience before a dream gets fulfilled.

The Midheaven or sign that falls on the cusp of the tenth house on the birth chart wheel often shows us what type of career possibilities might bring success. For example, someone with Pisces on the tenth house cusp may be interested in careers where they can help others who are struggling with emotional issues, depression, or physical disabilities and need psychological support. Various types of healing like massage, Reiki, or nursing could be of interest. The field of psychology and social work might be appealing. There can be interests in art, music, writing, or entertainment as well. Working in astrology or another metaphysical profession may be a calling. A pull toward the helping professions can be linked to Neptune in the tenth house. Planet placements in this house bring a practical approach, sense of purpose, and mission to have a visible public life. Developing connections with others and business partnerships can help promote your career advancement. This house is important in helping you find your place in the world and feeling appreciated for the work you do. There is no greater feeling than working in a job you love while feeling the respect of your clients, supervisor, co-workers, and colleagues.

The Eleventh House: Aquarius

This is the land of freedom and true individuality. Your mind is likely trendsetting when you discover your passion resides here. You probably enjoy a wide circle of friends. Those who support your goals have a special place in your heart. Working with groups, social networking, and developing a team are important for any organization. Anytime more than two individuals meet together for a common goal, we need to thank the eleventh house. The airy eleventh house is often associated with friendship and acquaintances but most importantly rules group behavior and humanitarian causes. Aquarius is the sign that rules the eleventh, and there is a tendency to form relationships that are more platonic and based on friendship, although it should be said someone looking for a friend and lover in the same person can be linked to this house. The energy traveling through this terrain is intellectual and often not emotional. Both the eleventh house and Aquarius, the eleventh zodiac sign, are known for their coolness, aloofness, and detachment from emotions. Those with strong eleventh house energy can tend to intellectualize because they have an extremely mental approach in relating to others.

The eleventh house instills a humanitarian philosophy that involves helping people in a practical way. The Peace Corps and AmeriCorps, organizations that seek to help large groups of people on a broader scale, fall under this house. The eleventh house offers the uncanny ability to listen to people's difficulties without taking on those problems. This landscape gives each of us emotional boundaries. The energy of this house is about helping others on a small or large scale in a detached, logical, practical way and teaching skills to others to help themselves. Those with a strong eleventh house will open their hearts and support loved ones.

When you have planets in the eleventh house, you may feel a desire to be a part of a group and may prefer to join organizations rather than working alone. Then again, the independent streak of an eleventh house presence can show someone who is not comfortable with a group involvement for long periods of time. The freedom element rings extra loud in this terrain.

The energy of this house can manifest a mission of service that involves socializing, organizing, and developing connections with a wide range of acquaintances. People with planets in the eleventh house usually attract a diverse group of friends. Creativity and thinking outside of the box are important in the eleventh house atmosphere. There is a need to stand out from the crowd and be seen as different from others.

When planets are placed here, you may want to join groups that have a unique mission. Individuals with unconventional minds or controversial behavior may seem intriguing. Nontraditional thinking is an eleventh house trait. Therefore, activities that open people's minds such as joining a UFO club, working with AIDS patients, or rallying for animal rights relate to this house. Working with groups and developing lasting friendships with others is the key to eleventh house success. Walking to your own drumbeat is the rhythm of the eleventh house.

The Twelfth House: Pisces

This is the house of big dreams. The twelfth house can lift our imagination to new heights if we keep our expectations reasonable. Imagine feeling a higher power's presence touch your heart and soul. Some individuals are lucky to feel such an emotion, and they could have a few planets in the twelfth house or at least have found a way to tap into this fountain of intuition. This house features escapism, intuition, compassion, cosmic consciousness, loneliness, service to others, suffering, psychological issues, and secrets. Does this sound like a complicated place? Don't worry. The upside is there is an endless watery ocean of creativity flowing here.

While personal suffering, broken hearts, and loneliness can surface through this terrain, powerful experiences of spirituality and belief in your dreams reside here as well. Like the authors of this book, many healers and empaths are influenced by the mystical twelfth. Merlin likely knew this energy as a strong ally during the days of King Arthur. You can attract people with similar beliefs who believe in you through this cosmic connecting sky. The truth is that this watery house is the most mystical one in your natal chart. Twelfth house energy is angelic and showers us with compassion. The twelfth house rules psychic and mystical experiences. Some view this house as both a blessing and a curse because you will have to face many deep experiences if you have planets here. Like the character in the song "Hotel California" by the rock group the Eagles, you may wonder if you're in heaven or Hades. This only means that the twelfth house can reveal deep parts of our inner world. There is really nothing to fear because the universe tries to uplift us out of our shadows through this miraculous house. Feeling things deeply or understanding life in a way that most people don't happens when planets are here. Twelfth house energy allows us to feel different—sometimes like an alien and not from this earth. A theory suggests that the twelfth house sensitizes us to the energy of others and to outside stimuli.

At times, those with planets in the twelfth house experience a strong urge to spend time alone—almost like the Native American vision quest to have new illuminating insights. The energy of this house can turn us inward. It creates a safe, reclusive, private inner home for recharging. But there are exceptions to this aloneness. The twelfth house also can instill the drive to make a dream come true. Believing in your own ability accomplishes wonderful things. Creative individuals are often expressing energy from this mothership of an intuitive sacred oasis.

When the Sun is in the twelfth house, for example, you may want to withdraw from the world when you feel stressed. With some rest and relaxation, a person can hit the ground running again. You can feel depressed or sad at times for no apparent reason because you are experiencing a mystical type of processing to give you a clearer awareness. You may feel strange during this interlude, but eventually you know you are mentally and emotionally stronger.

Twelfth house people attract those with emotional problems because planets in this house create a magnetic field around us that draws wounded souls seeking comfort. Developing boundaries is vital in order to maintain a clear sense of how much help you actually can give to others. Staying in denial about our own needs, happiness, comfort, and emotional safety gets us into trouble in relationships. Our own reality-testing in a relationship must stay vibrant. Finding an equal give and take in partnerships is the road to harmony.

Self-care is important when planets are in the twelfth. We can thank the sign Pisces, the ruler of the twelfth house, for this great gift. Pisces is the mystic sign and shares this trait with the twelfth house. Escapism and compassion go hand in hand with the twelfth house. There is a tendency to overindulge in alcohol, food, or sleep when a person feels emotionally lost. Sometimes it only takes a stronger belief in yourself or help from caring others to turn this behavior into positive life pursuits. Meditation and internal reflection can be allies when it comes to getting healed. Staying grounded mentally is essential.

When planets are in the twelfth house, we often deal with issues surrounding personal boundaries. If there are no clear boundaries, our dependency needs get out of balance. Each of us needs self-care to protect ourselves from burnout and too much stress. The twelfth house encourages us to seek a connection to a higher power. Through tuning into our highest beliefs and spirituality, the twelfth house gives a sense of belonging and protection. Through meditation, positive thinking, and prayer, twelfth house people can find peace within themselves and a constant sense of purpose.

Part Two

The Magical Nodes of the Moon

Past Lives

To understand the power of the Moon's nodes, you have to be open-minded to the idea that we live multiple lives. What does this mean? We live in a current incarnation, but themes from other lives we have lived can influence our decision-making processes. Believing in past lives is central to analyzing the nodes of the Moon. The south node sign of the Moon shows your deeper soul personality and lessons learned from the past. The north node shows the type of personality traits you are meant to master in this current lifetime. A key thing to remember is balancing the magnetic pull of both nodes. When they work together in harmony, life seems more rewarding and filled with abundance. Too many astrologers think of the south node as energy to avoid. This causes confusion. In facing the shadows of our past lives as symbolized by the south node, we find personal empowerment and creative fulfillment. We recommend reading everything you can about the astrological sign and house placement of your north and south nodes because they contain much information about your personality traits. You came into this incarnation to gain clarity about both the north and south nodes. Practice learning to be more like the north node sign and have an awareness of the south node sign. Embrace the personality traits of the north node and learn how to navigate the tendencies of the south node. If you do, it will help you move faster towards your destiny and soul mission promised to you for this lifetime.

Saturn Return

Saturn is the planet of responsibilities, karma, discipline, structure, commitment, and career aspirations. In mythology, Saturn was Chronos, the god of time. In many ways Saturn works like a cosmic chiropractor pointing to how we might need to make life adjustments in our thinking. Most astrologers view it as a serious planetary energy. In astronomy, Saturn has rings around it that we can imagine being a kind of protective barrier. In astrology, Saturn symbolizes how we may guard our feelings until we trust someone. The focusing power of this planet can guide us to accomplish our goals.

What is the Saturn return? This planet takes about 27–30 years to return to where it was located when we were born (where it was in our birth chart). Everyone on earth will experience a first Saturn return between the ages of 28 and 30. Usually we first start feeling this energy around age 28. For the first time in our lives, we may begin to sense the pull towards our soul mission and north node energy in new ways.

Prior to the Saturn return, we are living in our south node where we feel comfortable. Things may feel like they are changing during our first Saturn return. The universe may offer us new insights. You may discover a need to reality test some of the choices you have made. Rethinking goals is a common occurrence. During this time many people experience major life changes. People marry, divorce, have a child, relocate, buy a home, or change careers. For instance, Carmen had a client who got married, had a new baby, and moved across the world during her Saturn return. If you talk to your friends and family about this age period, many of them will validate these important shifts in their lives. It's a time of challenge but also a period of great maturation and rebirth. So many people experience the transformations and healing lessons of this critical time.

Once we turn 31, we feel like a weight has been lifted off our shoulders. We begin to feel better emotionally, and life settles down a bit. We start to embrace this energy and move forward into this new phase of our lives. Prior to this, we could have been living more in our south node where we felt comfortable. The south node contains subconscious energies from the past of this life or strong influences from past lives that can resurface. Now we are for the first time feeling a stronger pull towards our north node, our true destiny.

During the period between ages 58 and 60, we experience this energy again through a second Saturn return. But this time we often find we already have mastered our north node sign and house energies. It might seem your south node has found a way to work in harmony with your north node. We are doing what we came here to do. The universe will naturally push us into our north node and bring in those south node energies more clearly. We can move forward willingly or go kicking and screaming.

Astronomers say that if Saturn fell from the sky, it is light enough to float on an ocean down here on Earth. Perhaps this is a good omen that our intuition can tap into the better, more flexible energy of Saturn and experience the best that our north and south nodes have to offer.

How to Calculate Your North Node and South Node

To use this book, it's important that you know how to calculate your own birth chart. You will need your date of birth, exact time of birth (a.m. or p.m.), and city, state, and country of birth. You can visit www.astro.com to calculate a free birth wheel. There are various online sites where you can input your birth information and obtain a free birth chart. Once you do that, you will be able to find what astrological sign and house your north and south nodes are in. This will provide highly valuable information and reveal your soul's true purpose in this lifetime and what you came here to learn.

The North Node and South Node

The Moon's nodes or lunar nodes are also called the nodes of destiny. They are calculated points in the sky where the Moon and Sun cross paths. Every year and a half, the Moon's nodes change astrological signs. This reveals to us our past and what our destiny and focus should be. In each of the following chapters, we will discuss healing tips for each node position. These practical tips can be used during difficult times to help you focus on the positive side of life experiences. In each chapter, we will discuss tips for letting go of stagnant energy and how you can learn from the past. All those things that hold us back need to be understood and released once and for all. Be patient as it takes practice to get good at doing this. A key goal of this book is to help you channel energy that has not worked productively into a more creative experience.

In Western astrology, which is also referred to as tropical astrology, the north node, also called the "true node," is a symbol that looks like a horseshoe with the arch on top. The south node symbol looks like an upside-down horseshoe. Some astrologers describe these glyphs as headphones. In Vedic or sidereal astrology, the north node or "Rahu" is called the mouth of the serpent, and the south node or "Ketu" is referred to as the tail of the serpent. It is also known as the head and tail of the dragon.

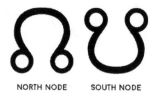

NORTH NODE   SOUTH NODE

Below is a sample birth chart wheel.

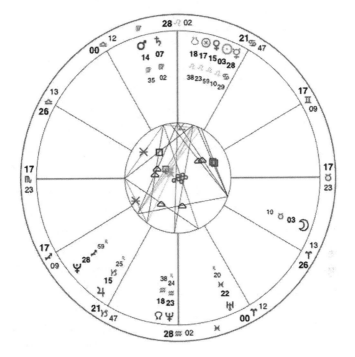

In the sample chart above, this individual has the north node in the sign Aquarius in the third house. They have the south node in Leo in the ninth house.

Carmen Turner Schott's Personal Nodes Experience

My north node is in the sign Scorpio and south node is in Taurus. I remember reading about these nodes in several books when I first started studying astrology. I was afraid of the intensity of what these books said my soul had to go through. Some books even referred to these as the most painful nodes in astrology. I remember feeling scared of the future experiences I might have.

I will say my journey in learning to leave behind stubborn, comfort-loving Taurus traits has been challenging. Security, safety, and comfort felt good. I disliked change and liked to know what would happen in the future. I knew I had to master Scorpio personality traits and release my comfort-loving ways. I remember thinking, "How will I ever become a Scorpio?" It was so opposite to how I felt and handled life. Over time, everything happened to test me. I had profound experiences with the death of those closest to me starting at a young age. Tragedy, crisis, and unexpected loss forced me to realize the fragility of life and that I really don't have control over anything.

Everything in this world changes and dies. Rebirth has been a constant part of my life. The greatest lesson I have learned from my north node in Scorpio is the powerful healing that comes with letting go. Not only have I had to learn to forgive others, discovering how to forgive myself also has been a powerful lesson.

I believe the life experiences I have endured have made me a better astrologer, counselor, and writer. This is the magical energy of the Nodes of the Moon as they weave their way through our consciousness, deepening our soul growth and allowing us to see through eyes filled with new rewarding insights.

Bernie Ashman's Personal Nodes Experience

My north node is in Taurus, and I have the south node in Scorpio. In many ways as a child and even as a teenager, I had trouble verbalizing what I was feeling about people even though my perceptions were clear. I was overwhelmed by the introspective, watery south node in Scorpio as it took me deep into myself. In my twenties, I discovered meditation and started on a spiritual search. I discovered astrology during this time. Reading and learning about the nodes of the Moon fascinated me. I gradually moved into my north node in Taurus and grew comfortable with my inner self. As I came out of the shadows of the south node in Scorpio, I felt a new sense of empowerment. Scorpio is linked to feeling passion, which I channeled powerfully into my interest in psychology and astrology. Taurus is connected to self-esteem, and mine quickly got stronger.

Each of us can find our way to balance this dynamic energy symbolized by our nodes of the Moon. A Scorpio south node indicates a person will experience their fair share of rebirths in a lifetime. This has been true for me. By making peace with my nodes of the Moon, my relationships and creative energy have been deeply rewarding!

Chapter One

The Aries and Libra Nodes of the Moon

Symbols: Ram (Aries) and Scales (Libra)
Elements: Fire (Aries) and Air (Libra)
Ruling Planets: Mars (Aries) and Venus (Libra)
Mastered Traits: Commitment, cooperation, partnership, diplomacy, fairness, focus on others
Traits to Learn: Self-reliance, independence, directness, action, patience with self and others

The Aries-Libra combination are the nodes of relationships. If you have the south node in Libra, you might have spent lifetimes pleasing others and focusing on making other people happy. When your north node is in Aries, you are learning to stand up and focus on your own needs in this lifetime.

In the past you have found your identity through your partner and through relationships. You must leave behind a tendency to overly sacrifice yourself for those you love. Living your life to please others will not work in this lifetime. It's time to make your own path. It is possible to please yourself and at the same time love someone else.

Your North Node in Aries

If you were born with the north node in Aries, you came into this incarnation with a strong need for peace and harmony. In traditional astrology a phrase that is often used to describe the sign Aries is "I am." The universe has taught you the value of relationships and partnership. A strong desire to make your ideas known is a natural instinct.

Having an Aries north node encourages you to take bold action. You are learning to be self-reliant, independent, and action-oriented. This is a lifetime where you may need to learn to be more self-oriented. Putting other people's needs too much of the time before your own won't work in this life. Using your excellent skills in compromise will help you solve problems and find success.

Success comes by being assertive and fighting for what you believe in. Believing in and trusting yourself is an important lesson. You have to get comfortable with speaking up for yourself. Following your own instincts leads you into new territory that helps you achieve great things this lifetime.

Finding strength by standing on your own two feet and being more self-reliant helps you overcome passivity. Moving away from always needing other people's advice, approval, and support enhances trust in your own abilities. Taking risks and following your intuition leads you to abundant self-confidence. You need to realize that you can make hard decisions and embrace the fact that you can't always make other people happy. Being nice all the time is hard. Give yourself permission to disagree with others. You already mastered seeing other people's points of view and compromising. It's time for you to stand up for yourself in this life.

Having the north node in Aries will force you to feel alive and crave excitement. Playing it safe and avoiding disharmony will not work for you anymore. Relationships and partnerships can't be the main focus of your life. You have already mastered sacrificing your needs and wants for your partner. Blessed with a natural ability to love others and be a devoted partner, you may struggle to meet the right person, or you might commit too early in life. This energy occurs to help you learn to be content with being alone. This is not saying you need to be a hermit. Find a way to be happy being single and on your own first.

The universe will send you the perfect partner when you are independent and free. It might take longer than you would like, but trust in the power of these nodes. You are learning to nurture and love yourself before you can experience this energy with other people. Marrying later in life sometimes occurs with this node but not always. It is also common for you to rush into marriage at an early age because you have a strong desire for love and partnership. You might have a deep dislike of being alone. Socializing with others lifts your spirit and can be totally enjoyable.

Developing confidence and being brave are important. Releasing guilt and feelings of responsibility for other people's happiness will help you embrace Aries' traits. This is a lifetime where you need to focus on your own wants and desires. Forgive yourself if you make mistakes as a result of impulsive actions. Trust your gut instincts and allow yourself to feel emotions. Understand that getting angry is natural. There is nothing shameful about feeling "negative" emotions. You are human and allowed to feel angry and use it in a positive way to motivate you towards success.

Use your skill of balancing and mediation to maintain harmony in relating to others. Tapping into your inner strength allows you to accomplish your career goals. Believe in yourself and know that you get much more done when you act! With the north node in Aries, you need to speak up for yourself and others. Fighting for the underdog and for justice comes naturally. You like things to be fair, but don't let that prevent you from making decisions that are good for your own life. In the past people took you for granted, which kept you from always openly sharing your feelings. This is a lifetime of learning to put your own needs first but also realize the importance of maintaining healthy relationships with others. Never forget it is okay to tell people "no," and you should practice this more often. Allowing this type of energy into your life can feel freeing.

Seeking freedom and independence is critical. Your powerful inner drive can get a lot done by being energetic, direct, straightforward, and launching ideas. The older you become, the more Aries traits you will feel. The universe eventually will allow you to find intimate and loving relationships. Surviving on your own must come first. Then all your dreams for love and partnership will come true.

When you accept and embrace the strength of the warrior energy and focus on your inner needs, the universe will magically send someone special into your life. This node might make you want to marry young. The best advice for some individuals with this node combination is to exercise patience before making major relationship decisions. Look before you leap. Waiting until you are comfortable relying on yourself financially, emotionally, and physically is the smartest move to make. Things will flow and you will start to see the energy shift, and you will meet new people. Relationships will intensify and grow. You will attract encouraging and healthy partners who help support you in achieving your goals.

Your South Node in Libra

Since you were born with the north node in Aries, your south node is in the opposite sign, Libra. In traditional astrology a phrase to describe Libra is "I balance." In past lifetimes you were blessed with creative and artistic talents. You mastered how to take care of other people's needs. In this life you have to learn to focus more on your own. In previous lifetimes you found much of your main identity through having a relationship partner. Marriage and commitment were important but sometimes blocked you from pursuing your own desires. First, you need to learn to balance self-reliance with dependency. Blessed with the ability to compromise, you are able to put yourself in other people's shoes. Always focused on the needs of others, you don't want to disappoint people you care about. You have a tendency to neglect your own needs to ensure you don't let others down.

At heart, you feel most comfortable when entertaining or interacting in social situations. You like to surround yourself with happy people. Finding a sense of contentment in your personal and work life is critical in this lifetime. Overwhelmed by strong emotions, sometimes you struggle to find balance. Intellectualizing emotions is common. Unexpected life changes create stress and affect your equilibrium. In prior lifetimes, you developed abilities and a natural way to stay centered.

Anger makes you uncomfortable. It is important to learn to express your feelings honestly. Peace and harmony are gifts you bring from past lifetimes. Because conflict feels challenging, you sometimes avoid speaking what you really think. Indecision plagues many areas of your life. Born with the ability to balance the scales, you always see other people's points of view. Fairness and fighting for what is right are important to you. Gifted with creative talents from past lives, you might once again choose to explore being an artist or musician. You may have a true appreciation for the arts whether or not you become a practitioner of them.

In past lives, you mastered the skills of biting your tongue, not communicating openly, and keeping secrets about how you feel. But in this lifetime you can't avoid conflict, and keeping the peace can sometimes be harmful. You are here to grow more confident in yourself and to pursue your goals. Trusting your intuition and gut instincts will help you be decisive when needed.

Entering serious relationships early in life is common but sometimes very challenging. Commitment, compromise, and sacrifice are issues that need balance. This node often shows someone will learn many life lessons through relationships with different types of people. You are not here to judge yourself or a partner if a relationship runs into problems that appear impossible to fix. Learning from past relationships can help you avoid having the same issues surface again. The biggest lesson to learn is how to balance your own needs with those of others. Sometimes you sacrificed too much because you desire to be loved. You can't deny your own needs just to please others. Extremely romantic, you often look for a soul mate. You might feel you are seeking something but not quite sure what it is you are looking for. Then again, you may find or may have already met that right person who understands and cares about you in the deepest way!

Some tips for keeping the north node in Aries and south node in Libra balanced in harmony and abundance:
- Trust yourself to make decisions on your own.
- Allow yourself to express anger and uncomfortable feelings.
- Be assertive and learn to focus on yourself.
- Make decisions that bring growth.
- Maximize your natural artistic and creative talents.
- Adapt to conflict to stay aligned with your soul mission.
- Choose healthy and supportive partners.
- Be brave and act with conviction as Aries asks you to do.
- Stop trying to overly please others as Libra would have you do.

Your North Node in First House and South Node in Seventh House

First House Element: Fire
Seventh House Element: Air

Mastered Traits: Commitment, compromise, harmony, fairness, peacefulnessTraits to Learn: Self-reliance, independence, self-centeredness, bravery, autonomy

The first and seventh houses are the nodes of balancing independence and interdependence. Overcoming codependency and indecisiveness is a first house lesson. There is a pull between being self-reliant and committing to a partner. The first and seventh house energies influence how you take care of your own needs and the needs of others. Each gives a desire to bond with another person and experience intimacy. You enjoy being around other people. Your need for harmony can affect how you express yourself. This may cause you to be indecisive and withdraw from conflict. Your ability to understand what other people are feeling is a gift. Being alone can feel scary. Your self-confidence grows stronger when you realize you can do things on your own. Learning to be single, becoming financially independent, and having freedom helps you find balance.

Your North Node in First House

You came into this lifetime to focus on yourself. Forming a strong identity and not relying on others to tell you who you are is critical. You possess a strong desire to bond with another person and have a relationship. If you focus too much on the needs of others, you find difficulty maintaining a relationship. Meeting people with whom you connect may prove challenging. Sometimes you feel like love is hard to find. In some ways it is because you are here to learn to be content with your own company. When you try to discover who you are through a partner, many things can go wrong. You must learn to be more independent first and focus on finding out what makes you happy. If you give advance warning that you are ready to trade in an old plan for a new one, you win greater support.

Experiencing emotions can be difficult. In the past you learned to intellectualize your feelings. This lifetime requires you to react, listen to your gut instincts, and feel things intensely. Developing confidence in your ability to survive on your own is a key to mastering the north node in the first house.

Your desire to balance many areas of your life can cause difficulty. You might have to ignore the needs of others and put yourself first. This does not mean you are selfish, but your soul is tired of giving away your energy and depleting yourself. Focusing on your own happiness first is the key to finding a healthy, stable partner in the future.

Setting boundaries and learning to be self-reliant are the key lessons the first house is trying to teach you. It's important to let go of wanting other people to like you and caring about their opinions. You are easygoing and make people feel comfortable. Listening to others is a gift you mastered in past lives. In this life, you are learning to listen to yourself and value your own opinion.

Your South Node in Seventh House

You focused on one-on-one relationships in past lives. You successfully grasped the art of being married and partnering with other people on a common goal. When you lean in to your south node, dependency issues can affect your ability to do things on your own. Sometimes you turn to your partner or seek validation from other people. Trusting yourself and developing more self-confidence will help you grow. When the south node is in the seventh house, in past incarnations you mastered compromise and overcoming relationship challenges. A lot of soul growth came through being married or in a committed relationship.

In this lifetime you still retain a desire to find love. The problem is that you already made that your priority in the past. The new energy that impacts your life involves forcing you to step out of your comfort zone. You have to take risks and challenge yourself to do things on your own. Doing things that are scary makes you snap out of old, outdated patterns. In relationships, you tend to attract partners who need your help. Sometimes you become codependent and lose your identity in your partner. Prioritizing your partner's needs over your own will only cause heartache.

The seventh house has taught you valuable lessons about commitment. It's time for you to step out solo and blaze your own path. The seventh house blessed you with negotiation skills, and you can help other people with their problems. Conflict resolution and creating harmony with others are gifts you bring with you into this lifetime.

The seventh house is about joining forces with someone else to find out who you really are. It forces you to sacrifice your selfish needs in order to support someone equally. When you find a balance between selfishness and unconditional love, you will experience the true transformation of this node.

Being supportive and making situations peaceful comes naturally to you. Determination and a drive to achieve goals helps you develop confidence. Trust yourself and let people know who you really are. It's okay to stand out and be noticed. You came into this life to learn more about being brave and courageous.

Some tips for keeping the north node in the first house and the south node in the seventh house balanced in harmony and abundance:

- Focus on your own needs.
- Pursue your goals.
- Get comfortable being alone.
- Learn to balance relationships with others.

- Companionship helps increase happiness.
- Maintain a sense of freedom.
- Make decisions and listen to your gut instincts.
- Be courageous, confident, brave, and self-assured as the first house asks.
- Focus on others, balance relationships, and compromise as the seventh house asks.

The Libra North Node & Aries South Node

Symbols: Scales (Libra) and Ram (Aries)

Elements: Air (Libra) and Fire (Aries)

Ruling Planets: Venus (Libra) and Mars (Aries)

Mastered Traits: Commitment, cooperation, partnership, diplomacy, fairness, focus on others

Traits to Learn: Self-Reliance, independence, directness, action, patience with self and others

Libra North Node

If you were born with the north node in Libra, you came into this incarnation with a strong need for independence. In traditional astrology a phrase that is often used to describe the sign Libra is "I balance." Fiercely self-reliant, everything you do comes from an inner desire to succeed. You feel you have to do everything on your own. Relying on or waiting for others to help makes you nervous. Acting, making your own decisions, and focusing on your own wants and needs comes naturally. In past incarnations survival was paramount, and you had to make difficult choices. You learned to be self-focused, self-centered, and indifferent to what others wanted. You valued your own intuition and gut instincts.

You came into this lifetime with unresolved anger and frustration surrounding relationships. You mastered how to take care of your own needs. This lifetime you have to learn how to have healthy relationships. Karma with others is a challenge; people in general are here to teach you major lessons. You need to remember that you can still be independent and allow yourself to have committed relationships. Learning to listen to others' feelings and honoring them will help you overcome self-centered traits. Putting other people's needs before your own is a challenge. Allow yourself to be vulnerable and accept help from loved ones if they offer it.

In past incarnations you were a leader and good at motivating other people. You don't shy away from conflict but need to learn how to become a peacemaker. Seeing the validity in other people's perspectives and nourishing healthy competition will help you reach personal and professional goals. This is a lifetime where you need other people to achieve your desires; you can't do it solo.

Making decisions and acting on your own accord can prevent you from connecting with other people. Angry outbursts occur when you don't feel things work out the way you want. You need to learn patience and how to calm your intense emotional nature. Bluntness and directness in communication comes easily, but you have to discover how to listen without always talking. Let other people talk first. Wait and then share what you think and feel. Passionate lovers, those with a Libra north node are learning to balance self-interest and the emotional needs of partners in relationships. Many with this node finds themselves single and often waiting until later in life to get married. There are lessons to learn before the universe allows you to partner. If you do marry young before you learn to express Libra traits, you will often separate or divorce. Legal troubles can happen to help you learn how to compromise.

Finding harmony in relationships and avoiding competing with others is crucial. There are fears surrounding appearing weak and needing to be right. When you compete with other people, especially loved ones, it can push them away. Being sensitive to your partner's needs helps relationships thrive. This is an incarnation of finding intimacy, commitment, partnership, and harmony in personal relationships.

Aries South Node

Since you were born with the north node in Libra, your south node is in the opposite sign, Aries. In traditional astrology a phrase to describe Aries is "I am." Aries energy is self-focused and motivated on getting their needs met. In past lifetimes you had to survive on your own. You learned you could not depend on other people to meet your needs. Being independent comes naturally to you, and you dislike being told what to do. Impulsive, you don't like to wait around. You prefer making decisions based on your gut instincts. Waiting for others to be on board causes frustration. You lack patience and want immediate results. There is a strong need for competition and winning. Sometimes you forget that other people have feelings too. You are focused on your own feelings and needs. In previous lifetimes you overcame struggles, dealt with crises, and survived on your own. Deep down you still believe you can't trust others, and this prevents you from connecting emotionally. Intimacy, love, and committed relationships can be challenging. Sometimes you feel it's easier to be alone. Moving on too quickly from intimate partners or using others in the moment can cause conflict in relationships. You get bored easily and seek adventure, excitement, and passion. You want to feel alive, and that means being impulsive at times, bravely pursuing what you desire. Learn to put yourself in other people's shoes and think about their needs.

In past incarnations you mastered being confident and self-reliant. There is nothing you can't achieve if you set your mind to it. Charismatic, charming, and motivated to succeed, you work hard and others like you. Born a go-getter, your motivation inspires others to believe in themselves. You need to be careful about being too honest, blunt, or direct because your words affect those around you in a deep way. Anger, rage, and frustration come pouring out intensely, which you often regret. Impulsive and quick to speak the truth, you would do well to slow down and think before you speak. Learning patience will help improve and balance all your relationships.

It is important that you overcome fears of commitment, being vulnerable, and feeling tied down. You can still maintain a sense of freedom, independence, and self-reliance when you are in committed relationships. Thinking of yourself first comes easily, but learning to put yourself in other people's shoes takes a bit more effort.

Some tips for keeping the north node in Libra and the south node in Aries balanced in harmony and abundance:
- Trust others and listen to their advice.
- Allow yourself to express anger in healthy ways.
- Be less self-centered.
- Before you make decisions, include others.
- Use your skills of confidence.
- Rely on others more.
- Balance independence and interdependence, which aligns you with your soul mission.
- Choose healthy and supportive partners.
- As Libra asks you, stop looking for conflict and competition.
- As Aries asks you, speak up and be honest.

Your North Node in Seventh House and South Node in First House

Seventh House Element: Air

First House Element: Fire

Mastered Traits: Self-reliance, independence, self-centeredness, bravery, autonomy

Traits to Learn: Commitment, compromise, harmony, fairness, conflict management

North Node in the Seventh House

Everything you do is focused on meeting your own needs. You had to learn to survive and figure things out on your own. In past incarnations you did not feel like you could depend on anyone. You have learned to stand on your own two feet. There is nothing you feel you can't do by yourself. In past lives personal experiences made you feel that relying on other people held you back. The north node in the seventh house pushes you to focus on other people this lifetime.

Naturally independent and self-reliant, you like to do what you want. Asking for permission and being held back can make you rebel. Acting, moving forward, making decisions, and choosing your own path comes naturally. You want to feel free to experience life and participate in all your own hobbies. This lifetime you will need to shift this energy and include others.

Trusting other people and feeling let down can be scary. Sometimes you believe that getting close to other people will make you weak or trapped. You think being in love may hold you back from pursuing your own goals. In past incarnations you were focused on your own survival. You developed self-confidence by achieving success with your own two hands. Strong willed, driven, and assertive, you can accomplish anything.

Sometimes you feel lonely, but you distract yourself by focusing on keeping busy. In past lives you had few relationships and preferred being alone. Autonomy is important to you, so intimate partners need to give you a lot of room to breathe. Relationships can be challenging, and you become impatient with others. You like the immediate feelings of being in love, the passion, and the thrill of the chase. You are attracted to people who are hard to get and like a challenge. You find it difficult to stay interested in someone after the initial passion wears off. Commitment can be tough for you, and it's hard to stay tied to one person. You cut ties when you feel vulnerable or if you are getting too close to someone. Moving on quickly and hurting others are behaviors you have to let go of.

Feeling free is important to you, but in this lifetime you are learning to develop and nurture relationships. It's important for your soul growth to think of the needs of others before your own. This will take practice, but you want to feel passion and excitement in relationships. Developing a lasting bond will help you learn that you don't always have to be strong. The best relationships often start out as friends.

In this incarnation, learning to trust others is part of your soul journey. You have to stop pushing people away and allow yourself to work on maintaining relationships. The north node in the seventh house calls for you to work hard on pleasing others and including them in your plans. You need to connect emotionally with a partner and give other people a chance. It is important that you find stable, reliable, and healthy partners. Your greatest lessons and overall soul happiness will depend on your ability to listen, compromise, and value other people's opinions.

South Node in the First House

You are used to focusing on doing what you want. You are uncomfortable neglecting yourself to please others. You view relationships as important for pleasure, but you are more content being alone. You feel alive when you are free and able to act on your own gut instincts. In past incarnations you flourished when you were challenged to survive on your own. You learned early on that you needed to be strong and courageous in order to reach your goals. Because other people let you down in the past, you push them away when you are struggling. In past lives you were comfortable doing things on your own and disliked being vulnerable or owing anything to anyone. Overly focused on your own needs, wants, and feelings, you have a single-minded determination to get what you want. Full of energy, passion, and inner motivation, you push hard to achieve success. Sometimes you sacrifice relationships, friendships, and family to pursue your own hobbies and interests.

You thrive on conflict and prefer it to peace. You are blunt, direct, assertive, and feel comfortable communicating your feelings in a direct way. High-strung, restless, and easily angered, you find it hard to be calm and relax. You learned in past incarnations that you got more accomplished when you did not include others. You see what you want and drive forcefully to get it. No one can stop you. You enjoy your freedom, independence, and ability to roam. It's difficult for you to listen to others because you trust your own instincts. You take the lead and get impatient if you have to wait for people. Following others causes frustration, and you like to lead.

In this incarnation you have to learn to compromise. It is time to focus on the wants and needs of those around you. Sometimes it feels like other people are not there for you when you need them. This can be painful. Relationships end abruptly if you refuse to open up with loved ones. You are meant to learn patience, diplomacy, and compromise and to be able to let others have their way. Sacrificing your own selfish desires will help you find balance in relationships.

You might have married early in life and things did not work out. Divorce is common with this node placement, and you learn a lot about yourself through these relationship experiences. Communicating effectively with other people and developing healthy partnerships will be beneficial. When you finally get comfortable focusing on other people and realize the value in relationships, the universe will send you the perfect partner. It might take some time, but you have to learn these lessons before you are ready to commit. Surviving on your own made you stronger, but now it's time to lean on someone else. One day you will find true love and a supportive partner to spend your life with.

Some tips for keeping the north node in the seventh house and the south node in the first house balanced in harmony and abundance:

- Focus on the needs of others.
- Compromise and listen to others.
- Get comfortable with commitment.
- Learn to focus on what your partner wants.
- Companionship helps increase happiness.
- Give up restlessness, impulsiveness, and self-centered tendencies.
- Find harmony in relationships.
- As the seventh house asks, focus on others, balance relationships, and compromise.
- As the first house asks, be courageous, confident, self-reliant, and self-assured.

Chapter Two

The Taurus-Scorpio Nodes of the Moon

Symbols: Bull (Taurus) and Scorpio (Scorpion)
Elements: Earth (Taurus) and Water (Scorpio)
Ruling Planets: Venus (Taurus) and Pluto (Scorpio)
Traits to Learn: Forgiveness, letting go, acceptance, finding stability
Traits to Master: Healing, transformation, allowing change

The Taurus-Scorpio combination are the nodes of transformation and rebirth. If you have the south node in Scorpio, you spent past incarnations dealing with change, crisis, loss, and personal growth. These experiences made you resilient and emotionally strong. When the north node is in Taurus, you are learning to embrace security, stability, and comfort in this lifetime. These are the nōdes of accumulation, letting go, and healing.

Transformation, regeneration, and healing are constant life lessons. You experience a pull between wanting stability, comfort, and monotony with times of change, growth, and cutting ties. This is a lifetime of intense evolution and learning to become strong enough to grieve loss and develop a spiritual outlook. These nodes are often believed to be more difficult than other nodes because as human beings we tend to resist change. Constant upheaval, testing, and emotional purging takes place with these nodes, forcing you to feel deep emotions.

Each karmic situation and challenge you overcome makes you stronger and wiser. Through loss, death, grief, and betrayal, you develop an awareness about loyalty, true friendship, and the fragility of life. A natural connection to the earth and deep spirituality comes with these nodes. In this lifetime you will morph into many different people as your emotional nature transforms throughout your life. These rebirths and emotional deaths can be symbolic or literal. As you grow older, you will learn the value of a spiritual path and having solitude.

North Node Taurus

When you have the north node in Taurus, you are learning to trust others, forgive, and release the past. Born a naturally private person, you can be secretive. Trusting others can be difficult because of the past hurts you have experienced. Those closest to you have not always been there for you or supported you the way you wanted them to. This makes you cautious about opening up emotionally or showing weakness. Extremely driven and independent, you do everything yourself and resist asking others for help. Vulnerability is a great teacher, and you developed a thick skin to protect your inner emotions.

You like to control situations and cut off your emotions in order to overcome challenges. Developing deep bonds with other people and experiencing intimacy through sexuality brings many lessons. There is a natural tendency to doubt other people's motives and see through facades. Intuitive, perceptive, and strong, you trust your own instincts. It takes a special person to touch your heart and break through the many protective layers you have built up. You experienced emotional extremes and faced betrayal in relationships in the past. Sometimes you have a jealous, possessive, and unforgiving nature. Once someone proves themselves loyal, you are equally loyal, protective, and devoted. Your first instinct is to doubt someone. Learning to trust others is one of your greatest challenges.

In past incarnations you experienced a lot of crisis and upheaval. Material things and money were not something you could rely on. Just when things felt settled and stable, you felt like the universe pulled the rug out from underneath you. Sometimes you had to pick up the pieces and start all over again.

Change was a constant theme in your life. This energy forced you to experience the process of rebirth and transformation. Emotionally, physically, and mentally, you were required to change in order to grow stronger as a person. Naturally perceptive, intuitive, and deep, you trust your gut instincts and feelings about people and situations.

In this incarnation you are learning to let go. Focusing on becoming more practical, stable, and grounded will help you achieve success. In this incarnation you need to plant your feet firmly on the ground and stay present. Moving on too quickly, forcing change, and cutting ties won't work. Pursuing practical goals and developing patience will help you attain greater security. In this lifetime you are meant to find comfort and emotional fulfillment. Forgiving others is a first step in balancing your karma and life. Holding onto resentments will prevent you from growing and finding inner happiness. Good luck and blessings come through finding peace and harmony and building trust in relationships. Owning your own home, having a stable job, paying bills, saving money for the future, and partnering with someone you trust will help you balance these nodes. Identifying your practical needs and minimizing emotional intensity are the focus. Finding ways to be calm and peaceful will help you heal past wounds and become more content with mundane real-world issues.

Remember that everything doesn't have to feel intense, rushed, and difficult. Focus on the practical world, and pursue a simpler life where you can enjoy good food, comfort, rest, security, and support from others on your journey. It might take time to fully trust others, but your life will improve once you develop strong bonds with healthy, supportive friends, co-workers, and loved ones. Learning to value yourself and others will help you appreciate the things people often take for granted.

South Node Scorpio

Since you were born with the north node in Taurus, your south node is in the opposite sign, Scorpio. In traditional astrology a phrase to describe Scorpio is "I desire."

In past incarnations you were intuitive/psychic and learned to see through the surface of things. You developed an ability to perceive people's secrets. People will see you as a magnetic, powerful, and intense person. At times, you like to control situations. Sometimes you attract people who seek your help with their unhealed pain, trauma, or problems. You have experienced continuous emotional rebirths where you had to grieve on your own. At times, you feel that as soon as you get comfortable in life, the universe takes away things you want to keep. Learning to survive on your own was challenging in the past, but it made you a stronger person. You developed a protective mechanism which prevented others from getting close to you. As a result of past wounds, trusting people is still difficult, uncomfortable, and at times your greatest challenge. Betrayal in relationships and sexual intimacy are areas where you have a wound that needs to be healed.

It is difficult for you to forgive and let go of things, especially your emotional connections and bonds. You probably have not attracted the most supportive intimate partners. Your relationships may have involved jealousy, power-control dynamics, possessiveness, arguments, and turbulent endings. You might have been attracted to people who tried to control your life, or you may have felt a need to control others in some way. Power and control dynamics were a theme throughout your life. Protecting yourself from loss was something you learned early in life. You dislike feeling vulnerable and want to have control over your own life.

Experiencing the death of those closest to you and subsequent grief changed you on a deep level. You learned to live in the moment and realized life is short. You came to recognize that each day is a gift. When things got too comfortable, you felt a desire to create change.

You grow bored with mundane routines and like to feel alive. Deep and insightful, you are highly intuitive. You dislike fakeness and can see people's true motives. You sense energy and the hidden things in your environment.

Naturally quiet, you make a great counselor because of your ability to listen to other people's problems. You give good advice, and your magnetic energy draws people to you. Protecting yourself by cutting off uncomfortable emotions or even people is a way you guard your energy. When things make you feel stagnant or stuck, you want to break free from that pattern of energy. Releasing, transforming, and letting things go come easily. The desire to heal yourself and others from emotional trauma might push you into career fields like psychology, energy healing, and working with helping others face taboo issues. You understand loss and can support others on their journey of letting go, releasing, and moving forward.

Some tips for keeping the north node in Taurus and the south node in Scorpio balanced in harmony and abundance:
- Find stability and comfort in practical things.
- Work towards achieving your goals.
- Avoid being secretive.
- Forgive others and let go of past wounds.
- Allow yourself to accumulate material things.
- Focus more on your values.
- Be more grounded.
- Save money for the future.
- Use your skills of patience.
- Balance a need for change.

- As Taurus asks, choose stable partners who are supportive.
- As Scorpio asks, balance power dynamics in relationships.

Your North Node in Second House and South Node in Eighth House

Second House Element: Earth

Eighth House Element: Water

Mastered Traits: Perception, power, intensity, transformation, rebirth, strength

Traits to Learn: Stability, financial security, patience, compromise, comfort, trust

The second and eighth houses are home to the nodes of healing and transformation. Overcoming a need for constant chaos, intensity, and crisis is a second house lesson. There is an emotional need to feel alive and experience upheaval in order to grow. The second and eighth house energies influence how you forgive and let go of past karmic wounds. Common lessons center on experiencing sexual intimacy, commitment, and transformative relationships. You enjoy owning nice things and pursuing your goals. Your need for crisis can distract from your ability to achieve emotional comfort and financial stability. You must master trusting others. Your capacity to be understanding and a source of strength for others is healing. Fears of experiencing poverty, lack of security, and having enough money to take care of yourself can influence every area of your life. You are strong, independent, and used to working hard for everything you have. Learning to stay present and resisting the urge to move on too quickly from people and situations will help you find balance.

Your North Node in the Second House

When the north node is in the second house, you have to focus on accumulating security and learning what is most valuable in this lifetime. You are on a search for stability, comfort, and balance of material matters. Working hard comes easily for you, but learning how to think of the future and not just live in the moment might be challenging.

In past incarnations you mastered the eighth house. You learned to survive on your own and found strength through adversity, loss, and traumatic situations. You were born with a natural awareness about death and rebirth. You are interested in deep, meaningful things and in the secrets of life. You already came to understand that your soul has a purpose here on earth and prioritized what was most important.

Deeply perceptive, you see through people easily. Others are attracted to your magnetic, intense, subtle, and powerful presence. Something about you may also make some people uncomfortable. You know their secrets that remain hidden to anyone else. This dynamic draws people to you but pushes some away. This incarnation tests you to find a balance between being secretive and trusting of others.

This lifetime requires you to hold on to emotions and find value in material things. You don't have to struggle or suffer alone. Seek to trust others and allow them to take care of you. Work towards your goals in a steady, dedicated, committed way, and you will find success. Be patient and allow time to help you achieve your future goals. There is no need to rush or push too hard. Allow others to assist you; be more vulnerable and try to give people a chance. Remember there are positive, helpful, and kind people in this world. You don't have to survive all alone. Open your heart and you will find a committed, loyal, and trustworthy partner. Soul mate relationships and past life love can show up when you least expect it. Look for a partner who is stable, responsible, hardworking, peaceful, and reliable.

Living in the practical world while avoiding intense emotional situations will help you find greater balance. Allow yourself to feel comfortable, protected, supported, and safe. Believing the universe will take care of your needs will help you master many life lessons.

Your South Node in the Eighth House

With your south node in the eighth house, your past lifetimes were full of crisis, transformation, and change. You learned to survive on your own effort. Struggles happened to push you to let go and embrace change. Your past lives featured unexpected loss and trauma, which forced you to be resilient. Deep down inside you awakened and realized that nothing in the material world lasts forever. Grief and loss changed you on a core level.

You encountered people who needed healing and often served as the wounded healer, helping others with pain that was similar to your own. In this lifetime, you may be drawn to psychology, counseling, energy healing, detective work, and digging deep to find answers. You learned to trust your own instincts and were psychically gifted. You may use these skills in your current lifetime to make important decisions and help you prepare for change. Forcing unnecessary transformation when things start to feel stable can lead to unfulfilled goals. It's time to balance your need for constant growth and finding security and comfort. In past lifetimes you worked hard to earn material possessions, financial sustenance, and to provide for your own needs.

The eighth house keeps trying to remind you to trust your inner voice and accept blessings. The eighth house is symbolic of the phoenix bird. You are used to feeling emotional and symbolic death, which forces you to rise again from the ashes feeling like an entirely new person. Having the south node in the eighth house attracts people and situations that are intense and transformative. It shines a light into hidden, taboo, and deep secrets. Your personal past life experiences will help you appreciate the little things that go well. When life gets difficult, the eighth house energy is there to remind you that you have survived much worse. Being reborn and adapting to the unexpected are past life memories that will remind you to see the positive in all situations. You are a survivor, and there is nothing you can't achieve once you make up your mind.

The eighth house is a spiritual and powerful place. It blesses you with inheritances that could be financial, material, and emotional. Other people often sacrifice for you in some way, or through your own sacrifices you grow stronger as a person. When you utilize your gift of helping others in crisis situations and share your wisdom, you will realize your natural talents. Taking quick action and being the leader in unexpected situations brings out your gift for immediate action. When you stay focused on building financial and emotional security through patience, you will find the support you need from your partner, family, and friends.

Learn to stay present, to plan, and to strategize your future steps. You attract your goals and find greater self-worth through trusting the process of planning. Don't cut people or things out of your life too quickly. You came into this life to find comfort and stability and to enjoy the practical things in life. Find out what brings pleasure and enjoy it in moderation.

Some tips for keeping the north node in the second house and the south node in the eighth house balanced in harmony and abundance:
- Learn patience and avoid moving on too quickly.
- Trust your gut instincts and perceptions.

- Avoid altering things simply for change's sake.
- Save money for the future.
- Embrace what brings comfort and pleasure.
- Stay present and allow yourself to feel connected to others.
- Focus on your future goals, dreams, and desires.
- Learn the difference between wants and needs.
- Build greater self-esteem and security as the second house teaches you.
- Connect deeply and experience intimacy as the eighth house guides you.

The Scorpio-Taurus Nodes of the Moon

Symbols: Scorpio (Scorpion) and Taurus (Bull)
Elements: Water (Scorpio) and Earth (Taurus)
Ruling Planets: Pluto (Scorpio) and Venus (Taurus)
Traits to Learn: Forgiveness, letting go, acceptance, finding stability
Traits to Master: Healing, transformation, allowing change

North Node in Scorpio

When you have the north node in Scorpio, you are learning to release the need for material things. In past lifetimes, you always had what you needed to survive. You worked hard towards your goals and always had a plan. Slow to change, you did things deliberately and stubbornly. In this lifetime you have to transform old emotions and allow newness into your life. Resisting change will block positive opportunities. It is important that you take more risks and break out of your comfort zone. Born a naturally private person, you can be quite possessive and strong-willed. Trusting others can be difficult because of the past hurts you have experienced. Those closest to you have not always been there for you or supported you the way you wanted them to. This makes you cautious about opening up emotionally or showing weakness. Extremely driven and independent, you do everything yourself and resist asking others for help.

In past incarnations you learned to work hard for material security. Your self-esteem was connected with how successful, materially secure, and stable your life was. You developed patience and were slow to shift; if you did change, it was more like baby steps. You are being called to transform and release outdated emotions, behaviors, and beliefs in this lifetime.

You are meant to embrace Scorpio personality traits. Letting things go, cutting ties, moving forward based on gut instincts, and trusting your intuition will set you up for success. Learn to trust your inner voice, which will encourage you to take more risks. Playing it safe will cause stagnation; it's time to do something new!

You can always start all over again, transform, shake off the dust, and move forward. You will feel lighter and happier when you release your grip on the past.

It is important to embrace new, refreshing energy. Waiting too long and being too afraid to act are traits to leave behind. It will take some time to feel comfortable with change, but you must create new opportunities for growth. The universe may shake up your life at times in unexpected ways. You're not being punished; these instances of upheaval might be a way to get you on the right path.

Loss, grief, and betrayal are life lessons that help you accept the north node energy and find balance with the south node energy. Feeling emotional pain helps you transform and become a more resilient person. You need to shed old layers of your personality. Look in the mirror and realize that you are not the same person you were. That person no longer exists. You morphed into a stronger, tougher, and more perceptive person. Accept the new you!

In this lifetime you need to focus on the deeper meaning of life and what your soul purpose is. Shifting the focus on material security to spiritual security will help you find balance. Making money and being financially stable is good, but it can't be the entire focus of your life. Spiritual and emotional happiness will come through deep experiences and having a spiritual mission.

South Node in Taurus

You are the master of patience. In past lifetimes you learned the value of money. Survival and practical matters were a priority because you felt you had to survive on your own. Focused on finding comfort and stability eased your anxiety. You sometimes feared not having what you needed. This made you hold on to things longer than you should have. Survival was something you learned the hard way, sometimes through loss.

Your childhood experiences helped you become determined and focused on achieving practical goals. Accumulating things came easily and preparing for a crisis became second nature. Your focus was on having material and emotional security. Providing for your own needs and those of your family brought contentment. Calm, patient, and stubborn, you could achieve anything once you set your mind to it.

You are used to seeking stability. Change and crisis were things you worked hard to avoid in your past lives. You were calm, peaceful, and slow to make decisions. Opening up can be challenging because you don't like to ask for help. You know others have their own issues, and you don't want to burden them. In past lifetimes you enjoyed art, beauty, food, and experiencing pleasure. You might have a creative interest like art, music, or dance. Surrounding yourself with beautiful objects makes you feel safe. You make a great listener and can offer practical advice. Taking others' advice is more difficult. You believe you are right, and very few people can ever change your mind. Stubbornness can affect relationships. Possessiveness and jealousy created difficulties in relationships. Letting go and forgiving others was a struggle.

Owning possessions helped you feel important. Your self-esteem was connected to how successful you were and how you could provide for your family. Affectionate at heart, you craved physical touch. Being outdoors in nature, working in a garden, or planting flowers was a relaxing activity. In past lifetimes you had a practical and creative side. Balancing both sides of your nature helped you find happiness.

Some tips for keeping the north node in Scorpio and the south node in Taurus balanced in harmony and abundance:

- Accept change as a natural part of life.
- Stay connected to the past without getting stuck there.
- Learn to trust others to build greater intimacy.
- Allow others to help you along the way.
- Trust your instincts and inner voice.
- Forgive and release as Scorpio asks you.
- Balance material and spiritual needs as Taurus guides.

North Node in the Eighth House

When the north node is in the eighth house, your lifetime is one of rebirth, transformation, and growth. You desire to connect to others on a deeper level. You are attracted to mystical topics that most people feel uncomfortable with like death, sexuality, and life after death. In past incarnations you were focused on building security and financial success. You are used to doing everything on your own, sometimes stubbornly. Taking other people's advice will help you achieve your goals faster and with fewer obstacles.

You need to focus on releasing your attachments to people, places, and things.

Sometimes you experience tragedy, trauma, or a loss that shakes you to the core. This occurrence teaches you to focus within for strength. Experiencing loss and grief helps you realize what is truly important. Asking for help can be difficult, and you prefer to suffer in silence than to appear weak. It's a strength to allow yourself to be vulnerable enough to trust others.

You always seem to have enough financially to support yourself, although sometimes you feel lonely. Fakeness and superficial discussions can irritate you. You prefer being alone than around those who don't share common interests. This is a soul mate lifetime, and you are learning to trust. Hiding your emotions and being secretive can push people away. You need to work on bonding with someone on a mental, emotional, physical, and spiritual level. In order to do this, you have to feel uncomfortable and take risks. It's okay to feel anxious, but you can't keep doing things on your own. You need other people to rely on. Sometimes you feel tired of having to do everything on your own and be strong.

Your personality morphs and changes throughout your life. As you get older, you realize the importance of finding a spiritual path. Researching the meaning of life and healing old wounds helps you build greater resilience. You have survived heartaches and life lessons that most people never have to endure. Like a phoenix, you rise from the ashes born fresh and new. Change is a constant in your life. Shedding old beliefs, habits, behaviors, and feelings helps you find out who you really are.

Material things will not be enough to bring happiness. Although you always seem to have what you need, releasing the desire to accumulate things helps you feel lighter. You will feel more alive each time you live through symbolic death and rebirth experiences. Focusing on the future will help you move in the right direction.

South Node in the Second House

When the south node is in the second house, it highlights past lives where you focused on building security. There were fears of never having enough and struggling in the practical world. Survival and planning for the future were priorities. Focusing on saving money and accumulating material possessions made you feel safe and secure. Surrounding yourself with comfortable furniture, beautiful art, and luxurious items brought you contentment. Seeking pleasure came only when you felt financially secure. You enjoyed good food, drink, and social interactions.

When you felt anxious, it was hard for you to have fun and pursue hobbies. Thrifty and strong-willed, you found it difficult to take risks or spend money. Extremely grounded and practical, you sometimes refused to enjoy life. You would hold on too tightly to material things because you wanted to feel comfortable at all times. Money and emotional comfort go hand in hand. You learned in past lifetimes that money brings power and prestige and opens doors. Being successful and working hard were things you mastered. You were a productive, dedicated, and committed person who worked relentlessly towards their goals.

Driven to succeed at any cost, you felt you could not rely on anyone except yourself. Your way of surviving was to accumulate memories and material possessions and to hold on to old, outdated emotions. In relationships, you were patient, loyal, affectionate, and committed. You struggled to let go of the past and old hurts. Stability and a rigid need to keep things the same prevented growth. You preferred doing things the same old way you had always done them. This behavior isolated others and sometimes pushed them away. At times, you found compromise difficult because it forced you out of your comfort zone.

Stubbornness and refusing to open your mind to other people's ideas caused tension. You were set in your ways and had a hard time listening or taking advice from others. In past lifetimes you focused on your own needs and pushed forward to survive. Relationships were often one-sided as you were not sure how to take care of other people's emotional needs. You shone in the areas of providing money, security, and a roof over someone's head. But listening, being open, and accepting criticism were difficult. Relationships were challenging and greater balance was needed to ensure that your own needs and those of others were met equally.

Some tips for keeping the north node in the eighth house and the south node in the second house balanced in harmony and abundance:

- Learn to trust others.
- Embrace new things and the unknown.
- Trust your intuition and act.
- Realize money does not always bring happiness.
- Experience pleasure by doing what you love.
- Balance your need to spend and to save money.
- Forgive others and release old emotions.
- Purge and donate unused material things.
- Be strong and resilient as the eighth house forces you to.
- Focus on finding self-worth as the second house pushes you to do.

Chapter Three

The Gemini-Sagittarius Nodes of the Moon

Symbols: Twins (Gemini) and Archer (Sagittarius)

Elements: Air (Gemini) and Fire (Sagittarius)

Ruling Planets: Mercury (Gemini) and Jupiter (Sagittarius)

Traits to Learn: Communication, adaptability, knowledge seeking, networking, teaching

Traits to Master: Focus, follow-through, listening, trusting intuitive feelings

The Gemini-Sagittarius nodes are those of communication. Both signs can speak ideas fluently. These are the nodes of socializing and teaching others what you have learned. If you have either node in the sign Sagittarius, you often will take the road less traveled. What does this mean? You want to test your goals even if they are difficult to attain. A sense of adventure has come with you once again into this lifetime. Being patient with yourself and others takes you far along the road of harmony. Having a node in Gemini puts a skip in your step to find those paths that lead to self-discovery. Being adaptable at times and focused when needed is a wonderful way to balance these two restless nodes. Maintaining clear perceptions by not holding onto negativity keeps your soul mission alert and growing.

Your North Node in Gemini

If you were born with the north node in Gemini, you came into this incarnation with a curious mind. In traditional astrology a phrase often used to describe the sign Gemini is "I perceive." The universe channels powerful mental energy through you. A strong desire to make your ideas known is a natural instinct.

Your soul growth thrives when you are open to the ideas of others. You are comfortable with friends, family members, and lovers who will verbalize their thoughts. Exchanging ideas with others stimulates your mind into creative thinking.

Reading books and investigating new subjects points your soul onto the paths that bring growth. You did not come into this life to be overly protective of a single version of the truth. The more you experiment with your creativity the greater the opportunities manifest that guide you to discovering your soul's mission.

Learning to listen to the input of others wins you important allies. The support you receive from people closest to you may keep you focused and centered.

At times, you may feel overwhelmed by everything going on in your life. Having ways to calm your mind keeps you tuned in clearly to making empowering choices. The universe has armed you with a strong mind that comes in handy when you need to solve a problem.

Learning to discriminate between the people who try to negate your goals and those who support them is vital to your happiness. The famous New York Yankees baseball player Yogi Berra once said, "When you come to a fork in the road, take it." For this current incarnation, you have been blessed with a mind that can spontaneously change directions and choose the right paths that enhance your soul growth.

The great Psychologist Carl Jung wrote and spoke about synchronicity, which he described as "meaningful coincidences." Someone like you with the north node in Gemini is at your best when you recognize the universe is putting a transformational experience at your doorstep. Embracing the magic that an altered perception offers you will allow you to tune in to messages from your soul.

Your South Node in Sagittarius

Since you were born with the north node in Gemini, your south node is in the opposite sign, Sagittarius. In traditional astrology a phrase to describe Sagittarius is "I seek knowledge." You may well have lived in many different locations in several past lifetimes. Archetypes of the sign Sagittarius are the teacher, counselor, traveler, and philosopher. Following you into this incarnation are strong instincts to find your truths in a wide variety of ways. Sharing your knowledge was heartfelt in previous lives.

Staying away from dogmatic thinking allows your soul growth to flourish. Life is more rewarding when you simply agree to disagree with others if your ideas clash. You are someone that likely was risk-taking in some past lives. Sometimes this brought great results. If you ventured too much into territory where angels fear to tread, you found great disappointment more than once. You may have impatiently failed to foresee the results of your actions.

Your wisdom gained from past experiences attracts people to you. When you stay away from overly judging others, you attract good people into your life. If you follow through on your promises to others, they love and admire you.

Running from conflict interferes with your soul growth. When you face adversity with courage, your soul does a happy dance. You have the mind of a writer and orator. Spreading your enthusiasm about your favorite subjects uplifts your spirit. There can be a tendency to put too much on your plate to accomplish. You are someone who can do this better than most. This theme followed you into this life. Just be sure you are not biting off more than you can chew.

Your ruthless honesty can shock others. Be aware your insensitivity can lead to hurt feelings in others. You stay clear of karmic impulses by not forcing opinions on those you love.

Some tips for keeping the north node in Gemini and the south node in Sagittarius balanced in harmony and abundance:

- Find rituals that inspire you and elevate your consciousness.
- Travel helps blend the power of these nodes into clear thinking.
- Maintain a broad vision but pay attention to details.
- Positive thinking keeps you above life challenges.
- Adapting to change keeps you aligned with your soul mission.
- Have a healthy respect for the past while living in the present.
- Communicate not to judge but to encourage others to grow mentally.
- Stay open to new, refreshing ideas as Gemini asks.
- Keep seeking truths not always from the past but in the now as Sagittarius asks.

Your North Node in Third House and South Node in Ninth House

Third House Element: Air

Ninth House Element: Fire

Traits to Learn: Passion for learning, adventurousness, strong imagination

Traits to Master: Expression of feelings, not being overconfident, focus, patience

The third and ninth house give us the travel nodes of the Moon. This can involve traveling to various locations or journeys on the mental level. The third and ninth house have a lively energy running through them. Each gives a push to express your ideas. You possess excellent communication skills. Your nervous energy at times can interfere with your concentration. This may require getting an exercise routine, doing yoga, or participating in some type of meditation. Your ability to adapt to change is likely strong. You detest boredom more than many people. Your mind works fast and can multitask at a high level. Learning to listen deepens your closeness with your favorite people.

Your North Node in Third House

You came into this incarnation to be heard. There is a strong desire to influence others with your words. You find it annoying when they are not paying attention. You are good at making complicated concepts and subjects easier for people to understand. In some ways your mind works like a reporter or journalist. When you change directions quickly, it either offers a pleasant surprise for others or bothers them. If you give advance warning that you are ready to trade in a plan for a new one, you win greater support.

You may hide your feelings. Why? The houses like the signs belong to an element. The third house is a member of the air element, which is an intellectual influence. You might find yourself holding back feelings until you really trust someone. This is not unusual for a north node in the third house.

Your perceptions about people are often accurate. You gravitate toward people who can share your enthusiasm about similar life interests. Those individuals who are generous in sharing their ideas win your friendship and even love. You may meet people important in your life in unexpected ways.

You came into this life to write your own story. People who know you best figure this out early in knowing you. Don't worry if this sounds foreign to you. You may have been writing your thoughts in a journal or have a secret philosophy inside your mind. One way or another, you are meant to find your voice through your most passionate life interests.

You are a natural advisor. People may lean on you heavily for your insights. There are times you need to retreat from the world to recharge your mental and physical bodies. Doing this is good for your immune system and keeps your mind refreshed.

You are an educator and an idea influencer on a grand scale. When you trust your insights, they empower you. Finding options for a problem is always at your fingertips. When you don't let details frustrate you, your path remains clear. Your soul smiles when you learn from the past and let your visionary self walk freely toward the light of higher consciousness.

Your South Node in Ninth House

Your past lives featured much traveling, sometimes to places many would not go. You encountered people from different cultures. In this life you may have an interest in meeting people from various parts of the world. Acquiring knowledge from others from different backgrounds may still be of interest in the current lifetime.

The ninth house keeps trying to remind you to think positively and find life paths that inspire you. The ninth house is symbolic of a cosmic lighthouse. This brings to mind a song by Pink Floyd called "Hey You" with lyrics that remind us not to allow others or ourselves to dim the light we came to share. The south node placed in the ninth house tries to lift you above any sadness and excess negativity, to shine a light into that part of you that is bold and confident. You were gifted memories of past lives to bring into this incarnation colored with endless rainbows of belief in yourself. When that faith in yourself gets too weak, the ninth house energy is there to elevate you.

The ninth house is an expansive territory. It calls to your imagination to never stop believing in the dreams you want to accomplish. When you find a belief system that motivates you, life feels good. In some past lives, there was a tendency to run away from commitments due to a grass is greener elsewhere way of thinking. When you stay the course in being there for those who need your support and love, you attract harmony in your relationships.

Sharing your ideas with people is an instinct from deep within your soul. You attract good luck when thinking positively. It is healthy to establish clear boundaries with others and steer clear of overly exaggerating your talents. Being a coach and advisor is in your DNA. You came into this life to find your truth along multiple paths.

Some tips for keeping the north node in the third house and the south node in the ninth house balanced in harmony and abundance:

- Believe in yourself.
- Trust your intuition to change a goal when needed.
- Find subjects of interest that inspire you.
- Let others speak their minds freely.
- Travel elevates your consciousness.
- Don't promise more than you can deliver.
- Stay open to new ideas.
- Be open to altered perceptions as the third house asks.
- Feed your soul with a mind hungry for new growth as the ninth house urges.

North Node Sagittarius-Gemini South Node

Symbols: Archer (Sagittarius) and Twins (Gemini)

Elements: Fire (Sagittarius) and Air (Gemini)

Ruling Planets: Mercury (Gemini) and Jupiter (Sagittarius)

Traits to Learn: Open-mindedness, motivation to learn, knowing your limits, staying flexible

Traits to Master: Embracing new adventures, avoiding judgment, learning from mistakes

The north node in Sagittarius and south node in Gemini combination share a common theme for desiring to move along multiple paths. Each sign has a curious mind. Boredom has no place in the world of either sign for long. New goals manifest for you suddenly with the help of this mentally alert node combination. You came into this life to make your ideas visible to others. Writing, teaching, and being an influencer in favorite areas of interest are well within your grasp. You may enjoy staying in touch with the world's current trends. Sharing your thoughts is often in demand by others, especially your family and closest friends. Positive thinking is your greatest ally.

Your North Node in Sagittarius

Being born with the north node in fiery Sagittarius inspires you to roam the world in your own unique ways. You did not necessarily come into this incarnation to always follow the lead of someone else. When you encourage others to confidently pursue their goals, you win a place in their heart.

Some might accuse you of being overly restless. You probably explain this as not settling to keep your dreams on hold. When you find a career or a goal that captures your imagination, you can lock on with great focus. Understanding the depth of a favorite subject can fascinate you. Your passion to express yourself captivates others.

When you stay open to the opinions of others, your relationships flow better. Learning to listen to those closest to you establishes trust. Patience may not come easily but can be a great ally to bring successful results.

Knowing when to tweak a plan and adjust to current circumstances is an instinct you were gifted at birth. Staying flexible is often in your best interest. To help you achieve clarity, at times you will pause and reflect before acting on impulse.

You show wisdom when not letting a lack of faith keep you from moving forward with new ventures.

Creating rituals that empower your belief system is a key to sustaining feelings of happiness and harmony. You may find yourself attracted to friends and lovers that motivate you to look for the deeper meaning of life. You came into this lifetime to seek truths that elevate your consciousness. By not fearing new paths to self-discovery, you find transformational growth.

Your South Node in Gemini

Your past lives are colored with having a strong and curious intellect. Communication skills were often in your DNA in previous lives. You often quickly outgrew any type of formal education. It was not that you rebelled against an educational system but preferred to study and learn through direct experience.

Focus on a single talent you possessed was a struggle at times because you wanted to move onto other areas of interest. When you learned to believe in your abilities, success was never a stranger. You can multitask better than many people.

You found receiving criticism a painful experience, and it sometimes turned you into a critic of others. You realized harmony was easier to achieve with important people in your life when being less judgmental. Learning to listen as well as talk brought those you loved closer.

You possessed patterns of letting your intellect too often hide your feelings. It produced a cold personality that created distance from your friends and loved ones. When you found the courage to show more of your emotions, the bond in your relationships deepened. Thinking positively is a mantra you came into this incarnation to remember. Negativity and self-doubt only serve to hold you back from a happy life. It is important in this lifetime to avoid buying into individuals filling your mind with negative thoughts. When you encourage others to believe in their goals, you win their admiration.

Enjoying the journey of life comes with practice. It is a key to your personal transformation in this lifetime. Not overly examining each step you walk brings inner happiness and a greater likelihood for creative success.

Some tips for keeping the north node in Sagittarius and the south node in Gemini balanced in harmony and abundance:

- Accept change as a normal process.
- Stay aware of the big picture without losing sight of the details.
- Don't fear going beyond your comfort zones.
- Don't promise more than you can fulfill.
- Be honest in your communication.
- Be careful not to overly judge others or criticize.
- Think positively.

Your North Node in Ninth House

Being born with the north node in the ninth house has the universe filling you with an endless amount of optimism. There is even an above average amount of luck that comes with this placement of the north node. The key is positive thinking. You came into this incarnation to dream big. There is an African proverb that says, "When you pray move your feet." This means it's just as important to act as to have your big idea.

You are a natural teacher and advisor to others. Be careful not to give too much unsolicited advice. Make sure you are not overstepping your boundaries in trying to help others. Your ability to see your way quickly beyond adversity is a special gift from the ninth house. Your belief in friends and lovers instills great confidence in the pursuit of their own life goals.

Travel can stimulate your imagination whether for many miles or a short trip. Being on the move helps channel your restless energies. You might be attracted to individuals who share your love of the outdoors and visiting foreign lands. Many locations in the world can call to your sense of adventure.

Education is something you probably highly value. Part of you may enjoy self-learning of new skills. Staying open to new ideas keeps you mentally alert. You can inspire others to think positively and never accept no for an answer when trying to reach their highest potential.

Your South Node in the Third House

You have a rich past life history of developing strong communication skills. With the south node placed in this house, you feel the desire to move in many directions at once. At times, you lost focus on major goals as a result. This does not mean you did this in every past life. Think of this lifetime as an opportunity to strengthen your follow through on important goals.

Positive thinking did not come easily in some past incarnations. You may have been too negatively influenced by others. You need to keep your best supportive allies close and those who have a negative impact far away.

Self-doubt can lurk in the shadows from various past lifetimes. Trusting in your own ability comes with practice. Taking small steps to accomplish your goals can turn into bigger ones with a positive attitude.

The third house can bring too much stimuli flooding when you get too busy. The nervous energy could have followed you into this lifetime. Don't worry. Slowing down to pause can get you centered. Meditation, even if for only a few minutes, can bring you back to a calm feeling. The main idea here is to avoid burnout.

The third house points to having been a world traveler in more than one past life. Travel paid big dividends in your past as it does in this lifetime. Being in other lands showed you there was more than one path to follow to finding peace, love, and abundance.

Finding ways to channel your restlessness leads to your creative power. On some occasions in previous incarnations, when facing adversity you gave in too easily to your fear. When you confront opposing forces in this life, you develop altered perceptions that carry you past obstacles. Success is liberating mentally and spiritually. When you stay flexible, life rewards you in a big way.

Some tips for keeping the north node in the third house and the south node in the ninth house balanced in harmony and abundance:

- Slow down and pace yourself to avoid mental exhaustion.
- Embrace new learning.
- Trust your own insights.
- Keep an open mind to opposing opinions.
- Enjoy the journey of life.
- If feeling negative, learn ways to think positive.
- Attract love and abundance by balancing giving and receiving.

Chapter Four

The Cancer-Capricorn Nodes of the Moon

Symbols: Crab (Cancer) and Goat (Capricorn)
Elements: Water (Cancer) and Earth (Capricorn)
Ruling Planets: Moon (Cancer) and Saturn (Capricorn)
Traits to Learn: Sense of security, trusting intuition, walking your talk, trusting others
Traits to Master: Overcoming the need to control, fear of intimacy, extreme mood swings, inflexibility

The Cancer-Capricorn nodes of the Moon are the nodes of establishing a secure internal strength and solid focused life. Having either node in Cancer pushes your emotional buttons on a regular basis. In many ways your moods are a barometer to help you tune into your feelings. The sign Cancer will guide you to find a happy home life. Privacy probably is something you cherish. The sign Cancer will remind you to pay attention to your intuition. There will be times you need some alone time to recharge your mental, physical, and emotional energies.

Having either node in Capricorn brings out your desire to focus on your important roles in life. This could be linked to being a career person or a parent. Capricorn attracts responsibility, so you need to watch out for becoming overly obligated to the needs of others. Commitment to a person or a job is an important part of the Capricorn node.

North Node in Cancer
If you were born with the north node in Cancer, chances are you value your privacy. In traditional astrology Cancer is known as the "I feel" sign. You tend to be sensitive to the

energy of people, so getting time alone to recharge your mind is important. This allows you to spend more quality time with those you care about. Finding friends and a lover you trust is essential to establishing closeness. When you share some of your inner world with others, it allows them to know you on a deeper level.

Living on a longitude and latitude in the world that feels right is something you likely value. Your home probably is a place that truly allows you to be yourself. You need a quiet escape from the world that gives you a strong sense of security.

One key theme for coming into this incarnation is to prove you can be independent. This is not to say you don't need anyone to be happy. You simply need to tap into your own inner strength because it provides a stronger sense of self.

You are a natural caretaker. Your loyalty to others is heartfelt. When a friend, family member, or lover supports your goals, your bond with them deepens. Individuals with the north node in Cancer often have a special place in their heart for animals. Pets can feel like special friends and in their own way bring out your emotional nature.

Some people may perceive you as secretive. You probably explain this as needing time to open up to others. Your emotions run deep. You often process your memories of the past right along with the present. You have a healthy respect for previous experiences. The challenge is not being ruled by negative memories so new insights can occur.

You find inner empowerment through the roles you choose. Your drive to do a good job is genuine. It is a soul-felt desire to feel needed by others. You can pour this into a career or any path you choose. You possess a deep desire to have the special people in your life recognize your talent. Finding a soul mate may seem like a great reward for agreeing to walk your journey.

South Node in Capricorn

You were born into this life with a rich past life history as a leader. In traditional astrology Capricorn is known as the "I lead" sign. This manifested in many forms throughout past incarnations. You brought these memories with you in your consciousness even if not readily apparent to your conscious mind. Responsibility finds you quickly. People see you as someone who can quickly take the lead both in times of trouble and challenges and when life is running smoothly. There are occasions when you will need to determine if a leadership role is in your best interest.

In some past lives, your competitive drive turned you into a workaholic. This pattern sometimes is your path to success, but you need to avoid burnout. Learning to find pleasure in doing enjoyable things either on your own or with friends or family members keeps you in balance.

Inflexibility is an old pattern that could use a new, transformed insight. Getting too attached to your own way of doing things can cause tension in your relationships. A tendency to always feel you must be in control will distance people from you. Letting the people you love and care about offer their own opinions brings them closer to you. The road to peace and harmony is easier to achieve when you show respect for the ideas of others.

There were past lives where you feared taking risks. Believing in your own abilities is important. Staying away from individuals in the habit of negating your goals is true wisdom. Don't fear asking others for support to bolster your self-confidence. It is not always easy to show vulnerability, but it might surprise you how good it feels to open yourself up for help.

Being a mentor for someone can be rewarding and may be a familiar path since you have done this in past lives. In sharing your heart as well as your wisdom, the energy of this south node becomes a great ally.

Some tips for keeping the north node in Cancer and the south node in Capricorn balanced in harmony and abundance:

- Try a new adventure.
- Change stimulates new thinking and awareness.
- Know your boundaries.
- Expressing feelings can be healing.
- Channel moods constructively.
- Support the goals of people you care about.
- Be assertive in making your dreams come true.
- Don't fear asking for what you need to be happy.

North Node in Capricorn

You came into this life with a serious intention to define yourself through roles that give you a solid sense of identity. Being recognized for what you accomplish is a bonus. Not panicking when facing a difficult challenge is built into your DNA. You have an inner strength that gives you the follow through to accomplish your goals. Leadership roles are often part of this particular north node package.

Willingness to compromise allows your relationships to achieve harmony. Learning to delegate some responsibilities to those you trust makes your journey easier. You bring the people you love closer when sharing your feelings. When supporting the goals of friends, family, and lovers, you become their hero.

Ambition followed you into this incarnation. Taking small steps to overcome a fear of failure empowers you. Learning to be patient with yourself and others is true wisdom. Being harder on a problem rather than on a person offers a winning formula.

Making time to reflect before acting could pay dividends. You have an inner intensity that drives you to quickly get a job done or a goal launched. Thinking a plan through may yield better results. You possess a wonderful willpower and confidence to pursue your dreams.

Capricorn is an earth sign and offers you pragmatic perceptions. Allowing your intuition to function as a valued partner enriches your life. The universe will reach out to you occasionally, asking you to realize you can't control everything. By letting the special people in your life know you want them to live out their own dreams, you discover a sure path to fulfillment. Helping to empower others gives you great inner satisfaction.

Whether they brought you happiness or joy, past experiences taught you important lessons that help you deal better with the present. By not repeating behavior patterns that cause tension in your relationships, you pave the way for stable and rewarding partnerships.

South Node in Cancer

Finding that right home and location to live is vital to your happiness. Does that sound right to you? This south node reveals you have past life memories of lifetimes spent on a quest to find that safe place and land of opportunity where you could thrive. Your intuition gets a boost in the water sign Cancer and may be a guiding force to lead you to a home that *feels* right.

You likely value your privacy. You may not share your feelings with many people. You may need time to make sure a person can be trusted. Your home life likely needs to be peaceful and feel like your castle. Family is something you often valued greatly in previous lives and could be important once again in this incarnation. You may not openly show your need for emotional support, but you appreciate it when friends and lovers provide it.

Being willing to communicate what you need in important relationships creates clarity. At times, you need to be off doing your own thing. People who understand this win your trust. Doing the same for those you love by letting them explore their own dreams brings them closer. Keeping your dependency needs balanced is true wisdom. You may have leaned too heavily on a lover in some past lives. On the other hand, there were previous lifetimes where individuals expected you to give too much of yourself. Finding that happy balance between give and take is the road to enjoyable partnerships.

You tend to put in your best effort whether it is in parenting, performing a job, caring for pets and plants, or learning new skills. You have a deep desire to prove you can accomplish whatever you set out to do! Your emotional intensity and passion will find their way into whichever roles you sense will bring happiness and fulfill your destiny.

Some tips for keeping the north node in Capricorn and the south node in Cancer balanced in harmony and abundance:
- Pay attention to the needs of others.
- Acknowledge the insights of those closest to you.
- Be flexible.
- Stay grounded.
- Accept change without resisting it.
- Leave your comfort zones to explore new learning.
- Believe in your talents.

North Node in Fourth House and South Node in Tenth House

Fourth House Element: Water

Tenth House Element: Earth

Traits to Learn: Feeling inwardly secure, confidence in your intuition, balancing dependency needs, pursuing goals with patience and confidence

Traits to Master: Learning to enjoy your journey, finding meaningful roles, expressing feelings

The universe channels pragmatic and intuitive energy to use through the fourth and tenth houses. The watery fourth house asks you to reflect before taking action, while the earthy tenth house guides you to find suitable roles that reflect your true self. Having your nodes of the Moon in these two houses reveals the need to be aware of your boundaries in relationships. Building trust with those you love is something you probably value a great deal. Your home and family life can become a solid foundation for your ambitious goals in the world. There will be occasions when taking a creative risk will yield wonderful results. Paying attention to the needs of those you hold dear brings harmony to your relationships.

North Node in Fourth House

Being born with the north node in the fourth house empowers you through your intuition. If you stay mentally clear, there is no end to how far your success in life will travel. Learning to let those you love into your inner world builds trust.

Many individuals with the north node situated in the fourth house easily absorb energy from other people. You likely feel a need to have private time to replenish your mind, body, and soul. It is important to value self-care.

There is a nurturing and caring side of you that other people may not recognize right away because you might want to get to know someone before you reveal your innermost feelings. It isn't that you want to be too secretive but rather that you desire to protect your vulnerability.

Going beyond your comfort zones is a key reason for your current incarnation. Embarking on new challenges is a path to personal empowerment. Getting support from friends and family raises your confidence levels. Doing the same for the important people in your life gets them to appreciate you.

There is a meditative part of your mind that at times will ask you to pause a busy schedule. Silence makes some people feel uncomfortable and even lonely. For you, the quiet moments allow you to peacefully process the past, present, and future.

You have a way of mirroring back to others if their life is going in the right direction. It is that magical energy inside the fourth house that works through you. This is a part of you that gets others to lean on you. You may need to give yourself permission to say no if someone is asking for too much.

Make sure you balance your work and home life. This is essential to feel like your life is in harmony with the goals you have chosen. Keep your expectations of others reasonable. You may have come into this life to change a few psychological patterns, but at the same time remember that you have an innate soul-felt desire to celebrate your journey.

South Node in Tenth House

This south node placement reveals your past lives took you into many different types of work. You liked to be challenged in a job in your previous incarnations and probably feel the same way now. You were often a mentor to others. Your learned skills in this lifetime may have influenced others to excel at their own work. In some past lives, you had to assume more responsibility than you wanted. There will be occasions when you need to lighten your workload and not be under constant demand. Rock stars David Bowie and Freddie Mercury of Queen worked as a team to write the song "Under Pressure." The lyrics to this song aptly describe those with the south node in the tenth house. You are self-driven to pursue a goal and need to know when to give yourself a break. Be careful to avoid pushing too hard on others to meet what you expect of them. You likely have a natural desire to be perceived as a reliable person, which could be a carry-over from past lives. People close to you don't need you to be too much of the time a type A person. Life will be more in harmony if you learn to relax.

You came into this incarnation to let go of the belief that you always must be in control. Your path in this lifetime is about relinquishing old psychological patterns that interfere with your happiness. When you trust your intuition and let life come to you rather than forcing outcomes, your soul celebrates your newly discovered wisdom.

You came here to establish solid commitments with those you love, which is not to say you failed to do this in other lifetimes. It only means you would be wise in this incarnation to give a relationship with someone enough time to reveal itself.

Positive thinking is another theme you came here to master. It helps release your creative power. Believing in your ability by taking that first step along a new adventurous path brings greater inner satisfaction and outer abundance. In more than one past life, you negated your positive thought processes. You can rise above this tendency by surrounding yourself with people who encourage you and build your confidence. Even meditation techniques are another possible way to leave negative impulses behind.

Perhaps you have heard of the "Law of Attraction," which is based on the philosophy that thoughts carry energy from our brain, and positive thinking attracts success in many areas of life including health, money, and relationships. A quick explanation for this is that positive thoughts bring positive experiences and negative thoughts have a negative impact. Your life journey goes more smoothly and becomes more rewarding when your mind visualizes the type of life you desire to attain.

Ambition is a good thing, but you need to watch out for becoming a workaholic and not paying attention to the important individuals in your life. Burnout results if you don't get the downtime you need. Balancing work and relaxation will keep your mind, body, and soul tuned to a higher happiness vibration.

Some tips for keeping the north node in the fourth house and the south node in the tenth house balanced in harmony and abundance:

- Learn self-care techniques.
- Celebrate each day.
- Don't fear success.
- Make positive thinking an everyday event.
- Create a peaceful home.
- Express your feelings.
- Make your intuition a close ally.
- Believe in your talents.
- Keep give and take balanced.

North Node in Tenth House

If you were born with the north node in the tenth house, you have an inner determination to make your goals a reality. If you feel hesitant to show the world your talents, exercise patience. Sometimes taking that first step toward success is the most difficult. When you begin to relax and trust yourself, life feels more flowing. There is nothing wrong with being a slow starter. The universe may give you a push to move forward in pursuing your dreams. You came into this incarnation with a strong purpose to clean up some karmic tendencies. Each of us has some old past life patterns that need to be resolved.

People are likely to depend on you in a big way to support their own goals. When you do this, it keeps your relationships with friends, employers, family, and lovers in harmony. You do need to know your own boundaries in how far to go in helping others. When you too are not demanding, it shows true wisdom.

Being flexible at times will come in handy in adapting to new situations. Life will deliver more opportunities when you are willing to pivot. If you start moving too fast, you may need a brief pause to consider all the options. Your mind can get moving in a hurry when your drive to finish what you start goes into high gear. Your perceptions grow clearer if you find a moment to relax.

If your positive thinking takes a dip, it is important to know techniques or ways to get back on the right track. By letting the people you trust into your inner world, life never seems lonely in happy times or troublesome ones.

The north node in the tenth house sets a somewhat serious tone. Navigate between that sweet spot of feeling driven by this serious tenth house focus and the parts of your chart that encourage celebrating joyfully. Such a balance is a true path to happiness.

South Node in Fourth House

Being born with the south node in the fourth house indicates that you very well could have lived in many different parts of the world in past lives. Moving from one location to another was likely. Finding that ideal longitude and latitude was a soul-felt desire on a grand scale.

In this incarnation you tend to be very particular about your living situation. Some individuals prefer to live alone. Many people need to put their own mark on their home or at least make it a place that fits their lifestyle. Your intuition can be a guiding force to bring you to a home, town, or country that will deliver the harmony and abundance you seek. You may highly value finding a community that matches your way of thinking.

At times, your moods tend to drift into a deep space. This can be your way of thinking through important decisions. The universe sends you new insights when you are in the middle of dealing with emotional situations. Meditation and quiet time can heal past troublesome memories and calm your nervous system. Not allowing negative thinking to bring you down goes far to ensure your creative success.

You possess healing energy and could have used this in past lifetimes to help others. You need to watch out for overextending a tendency to try to lift up the lives of others. Being a caretaker for others is a natural instinct, but living a balanced life protects you from burnout.

When you face problems directly, it has a transformational impact on your soul growth. By not fearing new challenges, you find wonderful personal empowerment. You enjoy starting new projects. When you follow through on your goals, even if you need to change their direction, it is a rewarding experience.

Feelings may seem difficult to express. Letting those you trust get to know you on a deeper level actually gives you a sense of renewal. You possess great inner strength that followed you into this lifetime. When you tap into this internal river of intuition, nothing can prevent you from a life filled with love and a realization of your paths to fulfillment.

Some tips for keeping the north node in the fourth house and the south node in the tenth house balanced in harmony and abundance:

- Trust your intuition.
- Share feelings with your closest friends and loved ones.
- Take time to reflect before making major decisions.
- Balance work and relaxation.
- Stop trying to be perfect.

- Learn to delegate responsibility.
- Don't fear success.
- Recognize you can't please everyone.
- Be sensitive to the needs of the people closest to you.

Chapter Five

The Leo-Aquarius Nodes of the Moon

Symbols: Lion (Leo) and water bearer (Aquarius)

Elements: Fire (Leo) and air (Aquarius)

Traits to Learn: Willpower, individuality, believing in goals, self-confidence

Traits to Master: Humility, flexibility, being a good listener, walking your talk

The Leo-Aquarius nodes of the Moon are the nodes of self-expression power. These signs can show you exhibiting a fixed determination to make your goals come true. In traditional astrology Leo is known as the "I create" sign. You possess an innate drive to find avenues that excite your creative energy. Selling an idea comes naturally to those with one of the nodes of the Moon in Leo. In this fire sign, your personality easily becomes dramatic and even playful, and you were born with a competitive spirit.

Aquarius is referred to as the "I know" sign in traditional astrology. Opinions can form firmly in your mind to make your ideas visible. Developing listening skills allows you to achieve a spirit of cooperation with others. Your mind likely travels fast with a node of the Moon in Aquarius. Patience allows you to make clearer decisions. You are likely a free spirit, meaning you like a lot of freedom to be yourself whether you are working or at home. You probably enjoy having a wide variety of friends.

North Node in Leo

You came into this life with a spirit that does not like to take no for an answer when you are pursuing a better future. Some people might even think you appeared on the scene of life to be a motivating force. Willpower could color your personality on a regular basis. When you are paying attention to the needs of those closest to you, it influences them to do the same for you.

If you have lost that self-confidence the universe sent you into this lifetime to embrace, finding your way back to this inner dimension of you is a key to your happiness. Leaving relationships or jobs that negate your self-image puts you on a transformational path. Making choices that bring harmony into your life promotes the growth you came into this incarnation to achieve.

Leo is known as a fixed sign in astrology, which means you want things on your own terms most of the time. Learning to adjust to change makes your life journey run smoother. You may need to learn to be flexible. This trait can come in handy to take advantage of a new opportunity. The universe can reveal itself to you in mysterious ways, offering new insights if you are willing to see them.

Many individuals like yourself with the north node in Leo have been gifted with an endless amount of energy to accomplish goals. Never resist having the courage to reach out to explore your most passionate dreams. By going beyond fear to believe you can make a new plan succeed, you tap into a type of rebirth.

Leo rules the heart in astrology. Finding a soulmate can be a heartfelt pursuit. Making enough room for a partner to pursue their own dreams deepens trust. Love remains strong in your life when you share your mental and emotional strength with others. Having this particular Leo node encourages you to make your ideas visible, and you appreciate receiving attention. Be sure to embrace the need for your lovers and friends to have their own thoughts recognized. Balancing giving and receiving in your everyday life keeps the doors to happiness wide open.

South Node in Aquarius

Your soul came with you into this life with a primal scream of freedom! If beating to your own drum is a constant rhythm in your life, the north node in Aquarius has a lot to do with this. In some past lives, your free-thinking self may have been thwarted by those who feared you. There was a tendency in previous incarnations to speak your mind and consider the consequences later. In this lifetime your unique insights often find you sensing when it is time to take your skills into new opportunities.

Aquarius is a mental type of sign belonging to the air element. Your feelings come alive when reinventing yourself. It may take some time, but eventually you will reveal your emotional side to those you trust. The inventor and trendsetter in you followed you from past incarnations into this lifetime. People who surprise you with innovative ideas get your attention.

Learning to follow through on your goals comes with practice. You can get in too big a hurry to move into the future. Paying attention to the needs of the people closest to you solidifies your relationships in the present. Finding a soul mate who is a friend as well as a lover brings much happiness.

Having your individuality respected is a sensitive issue for you. You came here to be seen as an equal in your current life. You tend to rebel against rules that feel too confining. You work best when given plenty of freedom. Don't be afraid to leave situations that are holding you back. The universe will send you a bolt of lightning energy when it is time to move to a relationship or work opportunity that better matches where you are in the here and now.

Traveling along the road less traveled is exciting and offers transformation and a sense of renewal that inspires you. Surrendering worn-out thought patterns that no longer serve your best interests is liberating. Learn from the past, celebrate the present, and keep your eyes open toward opportunities in the future.

Some tips for keeping the north node in Leo and the south node in Aquarius balanced in harmony and abundance:
- Follow your heartfelt goals.
- Share center stage with lovers and friends.
- Make adjustments if a plan becomes stuck.
- Don't become too aloof.
- Be open to the ideas of others.
- Stay in touch with societal trends.
- Admit when you are wrong.
- Don't give in to negative criticism when chasing a dream.

North Node in Aquarius

If you were born with the north node in Aquarius, the universe has gifted you with a free-thinking mind. You did not come into this life to always let someone else take the lead. You instinctively sense you must follow your own unique destiny. Life will surprise you with new, unexpected doorways to walk through.

Some people will perceive you as too aloof. You likely explain this as your way of staying objective about situations. Feelings are reserved for special circumstances. You have strong feelings about important events but don't always find it necessary to express them. Your insights about future goals can lead you to transformational opportunities.

Many individuals with this north node placement don't like to dwell on the past. You have a tendency to abruptly change your mind, which can confuse people closest to you. Learning to give advance warning to others when moving quickly keeps your friends and loved ones happier.

You are an individualist. Some will perceive you as complicated. Friends will find you pleasantly refreshing to know. Your love relationships become stronger and likely grow closer over time when you show you value the needs of your partner. You like self-reliant individuals yet at the same time want to be needed.

The universe sends you events that will stimulate altered perceptions. Seeing the world through newly reinvented eyes is exciting. There is an inventor in you. Putting your own style into your work comes naturally. Including the ideas of others makes your own creative thinking much more rewarding. You attract good luck when maintaining a positive attitude. Rising above negative input from others sometimes will be required to reach your goals.

South Node in Leo

With your current incarnation featuring the south node in Leo, creative thinking is never far out of your reach. Fiery Leo coloring this node reveals you have had several past lifetimes with a strong willpower. You may have had to scratch and claw your way to success more than once. Overcoming self-doubt is key to gaining a sense of renewal when you need it.

You came into this life to find a lover and friend who shares your sense of adventure. You thrived in past lifetimes when you received emotional support and someone believed in your goals. It is important you visibly recognize the talents of others if you want to keep them close.

You are blessed with a steady drive to make your dreams a reality. Leo may make you resistant to altering a plan. Being willing to adjust to changing circumstances increases the likelihood of success.

Your relationships are easier to keep in harmony when you avoid power struggles. Being willing to compromise and see someone else's point of view adds a flowing rhythm to your relating to others. You need to give and receive attention in equal measure with friends and lovers. Sharing center stage deepens trust.

Your ego strength must remain confident. You have a need to think positively so the Leo residing in your south node can guide you to a life of happiness on all levels. With this fireball of a south node, you tend to not take enough time to pause and think through a plan. Patience is an ally to utilize to get better results for your impulsive actions. Whether during peaceful times or tense ones, when you stay centered, the universe rewards you with insights that are based on clarity, humility, and love.

Some tips for keeping the north node in Aquarius and the south node in Leo balanced in harmony and abundance:

- Follow your most heartfelt goals.
- Remember not to let a failure keep you from moving forward.
- Asking for help is not a sign of weakness.
- Show visibly how much you care for those you love.
- Learn from your past to ensure a brighter present and future.
- Don't burn a bridge before considering your options.
- Keep a wide variety of friends and allies.
- Support the goals of those you love.

North Node in Fifth House and South Node in Eleventh House

Fifth House Element: Fire

Eleventh House Element: Air

Traits to Learn: Pursue your dreams, adapt to change, follow through on a goal, be patient with yourself and your closest people

Traits to Master: Trusting your instincts, expressing feelings, beat to your own drum, don't be too rebellious without a strategy

This Leo-Aquarius fifth-eleventh house node combination adds much excitement to your life. Leo does not like to back down from a challenge, and Aquarius will do everything it can to outthink an obstacle. When you put these two signs together in your life, sudden doors of opportunity can open. The trick is to keep your mind leaning in a positive direction with some flexibility mixed in. Doing so helps you feel like life is good.

You attract supportive and loving individuals when you give as much as you want to receive. When you don't demand to always have your own way, harmony in your relationships results. The other side of the coin is true too. You can't allow your own goals to be in a state of denial to please others. The universe responds in a big way to your dreams when you proceed with self-confidence.

North Node in Fifth House

You came into this lifetime with a jet propulsion-like creative force blowing powerfully at your back. This fiery fifth house north node colors you with a well-defined willpower. The key is maintaining your self-confidence to begin and complete your goals. You thrive on getting support from friends and loved ones. There will be occasions when others try to negate a plan. Summoning up the inner strength to make a dream come true can have a transformational impact on you.

People probably will depend on you for emotional and at times financial support. You will learn when to reward those making enough effort to achieve their goals and to hold back from individuals who are not self-reliant. When you find the ego strength to push through adversity, you feel like the universe has your back.

Sharing your life with a soul mate could feel like heaven on Earth. You probably feel neglected when someone does not pay enough attention to you. The same could be said if you become so busy you don't make enough quality time for those you love and admire. Balancing work and play keeps the home fires burning harmoniously. Being generous with your heartfelt love will always draw your lovers close.

You likely get bored easily. Finding things to do that occupy your mind is a must. Jobs that elicit your creativity and passion bring you joy. Your upbeat spirit inspires others to try their best to pursue their own life interests.

You were born into a vivacious fifth house north node that encourages you to walk your talk proudly. You learn quickly from life experiences, sometimes more than in a classroom. You excel at putting knowledge into pragmatic outlets. Learning from the past makes for smoother sailing in the present.

You are a natural cheerleader for those you care about. It is your belief in someone that wins their admiration. You need to celebrate your successes and stay positive if your goals get delayed. There is something magical about this north node that reveals the paths to abundance if you stay patient. At times, you may have to knock hard for a door of opportunity to open, but your faith in yourself will carry you through.

South Node in Eleventh House

With this south node in the eleventh house, you most definitely came here to experiment with many paths along your life journey. An inner restlessness will surface at times because of unsettled energy. You may get bored with routines if they are not balanced with activities that stimulate your mind. You need to reside in a location that provides you with many things to do. Having a home that lets you rest your mind is a must.

Learning not to worry so much about the outcome of situations comes with practice. When you are patient with yourself and others, life feels harmonious. Your relationships deepen when you give them enough time to develop. You attract people from diverse backgrounds. You have a natural curiosity to know what people are thinking and why they act the way they do.

You tend to rebel against individuals who seem like they are keeping you from exploring your goals. You can outgrow people and even jobs that are too limiting in what they offer. It can be important to avoid burning some bridges too fast before you have a solid plan.

You like people who are true individualists. They excite your mind. You came into this lifetime to reinvent yourself as needed to express a newly discovered you. This is part of the transformational energy of this south node in Aquarius.

Some may perceive you as aloof or too distant in showing feelings. You likely explain this as your natural way of living in the world. You will truly reveal the deepest part of you when falling in love or feeling close to a friend or family member.

Life will occasionally surprise you suddenly with an open door of opportunity. When you bravely walk through, it could lead to a life of fulfillment, growth, and abundance. There is a chance you will never look back!

Some tips for keeping the north node in the fifth house and the south node in the eleventh house balanced in harmony and abundance:

- Believe in your creative thinking.
- Be flexible at times to take advantage of new opportunities.
- Share your ideas openly with those you love.
- Be reasonable about what you promise others.
- Realize that expressing feelings is good for your health and mental clarity.
- Support the goals of friends and loved ones.
- Admit your mistakes but don't obsess over the past.
- Make time for your romantic partner to strengthen the bond.

- Balance work and relaxation.
- New experiences maintain your mental sharpness.

North Node in Eleventh House

You probably like your life to be filled with spontaneous experiences. An inventive streak regularly runs through your thinking. Your belief system is unique, which attracts free-thinking people. Having a wide variety of friends fits your style. You like much room to be yourself in work situations.

You find personal transformation by leaving your comfort zones. Don't worry. You can always return to whatever levels of comfort keep you grounded and centered. New learning explorations can bring inspiring insights.

Your perceptions can be influenced and excited by individuals with creative passion. People who give you a new perspective about your way of viewing your world can become special friends. Your unique ideas get others to see the world through a fresh lens.

New trends about your favorite interests might stimulate others to find a sense of inspiration. You have a way of stirring up the imagination of people. You may even rebel against the rules if they seem too limiting. You have the tendency to shine a light into the thinking of a group or an individual to expose their shallow reasoning. Learning to be diplomatic when disagreeing often will bring others over to your way of thinking. Being patient with those who disagree with you might serve your needs better.

You did not come into this lifetime to always be a follower. You cannot deny your own goals to satisfy someone else. When you are assertive about your own values and what will make you happy, the universe responds favorably with doors of opportunity. Why? Because you came into this incarnation with a strong intention to walk your talk forcefully. When you maintain a clear sense of direction, life can't help but dance happily with you.

If you need to change course now and then, it is fine. Consider this as a learning experience rather than a failure. Each of us at some point might need to reconsider a choice we have made. Editing your decisions can make them even better.

Believe in your insights, and your life paths lead you into lands of harmony. A lover who supports your most cherished goals wins your heart. When you return the same interest in their goals, it brings the two of you close in mind and spirit. A partner who is a friend and a lover is something you will always treasure.

South Node in Fifth House

You came into this life to make a strong and sometimes dramatic statement about your creative energy. If your ego gets bruised because people don't seem to understand you, don't let this stop you from reaching out to your dreams. Inwardly you have great willpower that can carry you across the finish line to reach your goals.

In some past lives, you craved attention. This theme may have followed you into this incarnation. Needing reassurance from others is not a bad thing. It only gets in your way if you lose your sense of independence. Being with people who support your goals and who don't overly criticize you shows you have gained wisdom. Your life paths find harmony when you believe in yourself. Your closest loved ones and friends will at times rely on you to encourage them to believe in their own inner strength.

In many past lives, you were a motivating force for change. You tended to rock the boat if you perceived an authority figure or institution as too controlling. In this incarnation this pattern of thought can reappear once again if others try to limit your options.

You are a fiery, restless spirit needing to find outlets for your energy. You feel more at home with life when you have enough goals to fulfill on your plate. Learning to get rest when your body is telling you to slow down maximizes your creative potential.

Finding a soulmate who shares your need for love can be a driving desire in you. When you are in the embrace of a caring lover, you feel great joy. You came into this life with an intense desire to seek someone who understands you on the deepest of levels. When you stay true to an uncompromising spirit to walk in your own footsteps toward a quest for new growth, you attract the best life has to offer.

Some tips for keeping the north node in the eleventh house and the south node in the fifth house balanced in harmony and abundance:

- Believe in your goals and they will come to fruition.
- Be a good listener with those you love.
- Learn from the past but don't be controlled by it.
- Trust your insights.
- Speak from your heart and reason with your mind.
- Be flexible to adjust to change.
- Channel restless energy creatively.
- Balance giving and taking in relating to others.

Chapter Six

The Pisces–Virgo Nodes of the Moon

Symbols: Fish (Pisces) and Maiden (Virgo)
Elements: Water (Pisces) and Earth (Virgo)
Ruling Planets: Neptune (Pisces) and Mercury (Virgo)
Traits to Learn: Developing boundaries, spirituality, enjoying solitude, service to others, and using imagination for creative work
Traits to Master: Being too critical, overanalyzing things, worry, controlling behaviors, managing expectations for self and others

The Pisces-Virgo nodes are known as the nodes of service. Those born in Pisces are focused on spiritual service while Virgos are dedicated to practical service. Both are natural at helping those in need. Establishing boundaries is a lesson for either node in Pisces. In many ways you're learning to balance taking care of others' needs and your own. The sign Pisces will guide you to seek a spiritual path and search for the meaning of life. Solitude is probably something you cherish. The sign Virgo will remind you to pay attention to the details and focus on the small things that matter. Sometimes you will want to escape from the stress of the world and hibernate. Once you recover your energy, you will be able to go back out into the world to help those in need. Finding balance in your life with being productive, working hard, and having quality time alone to recharge your mind, body, and spirit will help you accomplish your goals.

Pisces North Node

When the north node is in Pisces, that means in past lives the south node was in the sign Virgo. You learned the importance of being practical and focused on routine and structure. Finishing tasks, being productive, and organizing things brought a sense of stability. Having a job and working hard helped you reach your work goals. You concentrated on efficiency and disliked chaos and disorganization. Being productive and detail oriented brought contentment. In this lifetime you will need to shift to a more spiritual focus.

You can worry and analyze situations to the point of stressing yourself out. This can create more emotional tension in your life and can affect your health. The good news is you are a natural communicator and capable of expressing yourself through words and writing. Some aspects of life are out of your control, and you are learning to have faith and trust in a higher power. Releasing your need for control and heavy responsibilities will help you feel lighter.

Shifting the emphasis of your life from being overly focused on meticulous duties to finding a sense of purpose doing work that nourishes your soul is the goal. Balancing practical and spiritual needs will help you connect to others emotionally. You might be attracted to career fields like medicine, working with animals, social work, accounting, bookkeeping, nutrition, health, and exercise because you already worked in these types of areas in past lifetimes. You gained self-esteem through service and doing practical things for others. In this lifetime you need to be dedicated to helping others with their inner needs, healing, developing empathy, and nurturing human relationships.

Practical at heart, you are learning to trust your inner feelings. Work on getting comfortable with other people's emotions and your own. You're learning to be compassionate and balance expectations. It's time to make decisions based on intuition, not by overthinking. Tapping into your creativity and imagination can help you master latent talents. You bring a gift for writing and teaching into this lifetime. You can help your loved ones by sharing your thoughts and listening to their problems.

You can be high-strung and anxious at times. This lifetime teaches you to become more laid back and to let go of a need to control outcomes. You mastered the art of analysis and research. Digging deep and picking things apart is second nature. Sometimes obsessing on details causes additional pressure and stress. Learning to go with the flow will help you embrace Piscean traits. Shifting your thoughts and being more open-minded and trusting will help you overcome a high-strung nature. Set reasonable expectations for yourself and others. You can be picky and finicky, preferring things to be a certain way, your way. Adapting to change is a lesson to learn in this lifetime.

It is important to control your active mind and shift negative thoughts into positive ones. You will benefit from meditation, spending time alone, peaceful environments, silence, and developing stress-reduction strategies. Letting go of your inner critic and having realistic expectations helps you connect with your feelings. You have high standards, and it will help to embrace a more compassionate way of treating yourself and others. Don't be so hard on yourself, and remember that no one is perfect. You don't have to do everything on your own. It is good to ask for help or other people's advice. In this incarnation you need to trust others to support your goals and dreams. Doing things alone will not work this time. Learning to relax, taking a deep breath, and focusing within helps you balance restless thoughts and still your active mind.

Becoming a Pisces is all about being more compassionate and trusting. You already developed workaholic tendencies, but now it's time to balance work and relaxation. Releasing anxiety and tension helps you shift obsessive thoughts. Pessimism can lead to illness and block positive energy. Try to be more positive and practice gratitude.

You are meant to find your soul purpose in this lifetime. Helping others will be an important part of your journey.

Embracing Pisces means that you step off that cliff, trusting that a higher power will catch you and lift you up. You will find peace by believing you are protected and doing exactly what you are meant to do. You are here to appreciate the true meaning of service. Listening to other people's problems, feeling their pain, and becoming an empathic healer will help you serve others in an emotional way.

South Node Virgo

When the south node is in Virgo, in past lives you focused on the practical, realistic, and material world. You liked things to be neat, tidy, and organized. Change, chaos, dysfunction, and laziness are some of your pet peeves. Service oriented at heart, you can work harder and longer than anyone to get a task done. Accomplishing things comes easily for you because of your dedicated need to serve and to be efficient and productive. You like to see results and are not afraid to roll up your sleeves and spend long hours doing tasks that others run from. Sometimes you are so focused on the small details that you miss the bigger picture.

Analytical by nature, you will pick things apart and break them down. Sometimes you can become obsessed and fixated on having things a specific way. With the south node in Virgo, you might have obsessive-impulsive tendencies and repetitive behaviors. These repetitive behaviors might help you feel comfortable and secure in your environment. You are an eloquent communicator and possess a gift for writing and teaching. Even though you are a bit shy, you enjoy socializing with a small group of friends, family, and co-workers whom you trust. You show love by doing small, practical things for others. In past incarnations you found it difficult to express love or verbalize your feelings. Deep down, you are picky and notice small things in the environment or with other people that can annoy you.

Your pickiness, shyness, and fears regarding emotional vulnerability made sexual intimacy difficult. You might have preferred staying single in previous lifetimes and enjoyed your own company. Having a pet and surrounding yourself with animals brought comfort and companionship.

Spending time alone was crucial for self-care. You were highly intelligent and enjoyed reading, taking classes, and writing. It was fulfilling for you to master different subjects and teach others how to do things on a basic level. Working with your hands in practical ways in the past led to seeking work in energy healing, chiropractic care, or physical therapy. You developed perfectionistic tendencies in past lifetimes. Your high standards pushed you to be efficient. Conscientious at heart, in past lives you focused on pleasing others and completing tasks. You were drawn to medicine and healing. You found it difficult to say no or turn people away. Workaholic tendencies and neglecting your own needs could have led to health problems in past incarnations.

You mastered trying to control your environment but experienced anxiety and worry about small things. Sleep problems and overthinking are areas that need balancing. Release feelings of guilt about not being good enough and comparing yourself to others.

Some tips for keeping the north node in Pisces and the south node in Virgo balanced in harmony and abundance:

- Listen to your heart.
- Control self-doubt, anxiety, and worry.
- Build faith and trust in the universe.
- Develop reasonable expectations for yourself and others.
- Help others but also help yourself.
- Express your creative side.
- Trust your intuition and imagination.

- Find a spiritual path to follow.
- Make time for solitude.
- Balance practical service with selfless service.
- Connect to the divine as Pisces guides you to do.
- Serve others in practical ways as Virgo asks you to.

The Virgo–Pisces Nodes of the Moon

Symbols: Maiden (Virgo) and Fish (Pisces)

Elements: Earth (Virgo) and Water (Pisces)

Ruling Planets: Mercury (Virgo) and Neptune (Pisces)

Traits to Learn: *An eye for details, efficiency, implementing a stable routine, focusing on diet and health, working hard, organizing things*

Traits to Master: *Being too critical, overanalyzing things, worrying, controlling behaviors, managing expectations for self and others*

North Node Virgo

When the north node is in Virgo, your south node is in Pisces. In past lives you were spiritual, imaginative, compassionate, self-sacrificing, and empathic, and you enjoyed expressing your creative talents. You might carry artistic or musical abilities into this lifetime. Many artists, musicians, healers, and spiritual seekers were born with these nodes. In this incarnation you are learning to communicate and see things in a realistic way.

You are used to feeling other people's emotions. Many with these nodes are born with a sensitivity to the environment. You notice when people seem upset and sense tension and energies. The lack of boundaries between yourself and others can make you vulnerable to people who want to take advantage. People with pain and those who need healing are drawn into your life. You are the type of person who would give someone the shirt off your back. It is important to learn to balance a sacrificing nature by focusing more on self-care.

Your own needs are important, and you spent a lot of time neglecting them in past incarnations. You experienced difficulties in relationships because of your compassionate and giving nature. Some people might have taken advantage of your kindness. Communicating and explaining to others how you feel helps you connect. Standing up for yourself, being more assertive, and having healthy boundaries are key.

In past lives you believed in a soul mate. Seeking a deep connection with others and being in love were important to you. Extremely idealistic, you always focused on the positive traits of others. Karmic relationships tested your ability to trust others. Illusions caused suffering in intimate relationships, but this strengthened you. These experiences were meant to teach you to trust your intuition. The greatest lesson you need to learn in this lifetime is to trust yourself and be more practical.

In this incarnation you need to focus on finding a partner that is reliable, trustworthy, and practical. Balancing a need for romantic love with friendship is a new lesson to learn. Romantic and passionate feelings fade, but finding someone who is supportive, caring, and committed brings greater fulfillment.

In past incarnations you focused on seeking a spiritual path. You bring a basic knowledge into this life about mystical and mysterious topics like astrology, energy healing, meditation, yoga, and crystals. You carry spiritual wisdom that you can easily share with others into this lifetime. You will be asked to focus on teaching people what you have learned from personal mystical experiences. Connecting to the divine will come naturally, but you will feel a pull to learn to be more practical during this incarnation.

You need to master reliability, practicality, and organization. Finding a way to bring a routine and structure into your life will help you reach your goals. Being more focused and detail-oriented helps you feel more grounded. This lifetime asks you to leave behind traits of escaping from responsibilities and withdrawing from the real world. You must work hard for what you want. Your mission is to help other people in a practical and hands-on way. Living life with your feet firmly placed on the ground helps you achieve great things.

South Node in Pisces

In past lifetimes you learned to be compassionate, kind, and easygoing and to use your imagination to express your creativity. Romantic, idealistic, and trusting, you discovered early in life that you couldn't trust everyone. Sometimes you saw people through rose-colored glasses. Putting people up on a pedestal often created heartbreaking intimate relationships that taught you a lot about life.

You struggled to stand up for yourself at times and sacrificed your own needs for others. Being in love and finding a soul mate were the focus of your life. In the past you sought a spiritual path. You were interested in astrology, meditation, crystals, and mystical topics. Open-minded, you believed in angels and a higher power.

Helping others was a big part of your life. You're a natural psychologist and counselor. Listening to people's problems and giving compassionate advice helped you feel fulfilled. Sacrificing your own needs for your friends, family, and loved ones was a priority. At times, you neglected yourself and sacrificed your own wants and needs. Sometimes it was difficult for you to tell other people the truth. You did not like to hurt others' feelings and wanted to alleviate their pain.

Easily changeable, your moods fluctuated. There might have been times you felt sad and depressed. These feelings often overwhelmed you, and you might have tried to escape by using alcohol or other things to cope. Escaping from the real world came naturally. You experienced spiritual highs and lows.

Some tips for keeping the north node in Virgo and the south node in Pisces balanced in harmony and abundance:

- Develop a strong routine.
- Help others in a practical way.
- Be dependable and reliable.
- Develop boundaries with others.
- Avoid addiction and unhealthy behaviors.
- Balance your intellectual and creative sides.
- Have more realistic expectations.
- Eat right, get enough sleep, and exercise.
- Enjoy your time alone pursuing your own goals.
- Focus on your health and routines as Virgo asks you.
- Seek solitude and escape from the world as Pisces desires.

North Node in Sixth House and South Node in Twelfth House

Sixth House Element: Earth

Twelfth House Element: Water

Traits to Learn: Developing a practical approach to life and finding a healthy routine

Traits to Master: Embracing your compassionate side, seeking a spiritual path, and developing greater boundaries

The sixth-twelfth house node combination is about balancing practical service with spiritual service. The sixth house is associated with health, diet, routine, and work. These nodes help you balance the mental and the spiritual sides of life. Virgo is practical, intelligent, and an excellent communicator. The twelfth house is about connection to the divine, service, suffering, mysticism, and escapism. Pisces is compassionate, kind, and intuitive. When you put these two signs together, there is a wonderful balance of practicality and spirituality. Being of service, helping others, and alleviating suffering are lessons of these nodes.

North Node in the Sixth House

When the north node is in the sixth house, this is a lifetime where you are learning how to take care of people in a practical way. Serving others is your soul mission in this life. Learning to develop stronger boundaries will help you. You can't isolate or withdraw from responsibilities. This is a time to engage and connect with others in a practical way.

You need to develop a stable routine and learn the power of being organized. Planning and preparing to reach your goals will encourage greater self-esteem. It is important to keep going when things become stressful. Working hard and being productive will help you learn to be efficient in your everyday tasks.

In past incarnations you were interested in having a spiritual path and expressing your creative side. You used your imagination and intuition. Balancing responsibilities is important in this lifetime. Focus more on real-life matters like working, paying bills, eating, sleeping, and normal day-to-day events. Deep down you are used to detaching and avoiding heavy responsibilities. You are learning to balance your emotional and practical needs.

In this lifetime you will concentrate on health, diet, and developing routines. Co-workers, chores, childcare, and your employer are areas where you need to place your attention. You focus on taking care of others and might be interested in working with animals. Pets can bring companionship and comfort when you feel stressed.

Being more responsible and resisting the urge to avoid mundane tasks will help you find balance. Utilize the lessons you learned in the past such as relaxation, meditation, and breathing exercises to reduce stress and anxiety. You need to pay more attention to details and what is happening in your life. Paying heed to others and balancing your own needs will be beneficial. Avoid self-sacrifice and shirking responsibilities.

It is important to exercise, eat healthy, develop a stable sleep schedule, and balance work responsibilities. Focus on the work environment and build relationships with co-workers.

South Node Twelfth House

You learned the importance of seeking the meaning of life. In past lifetimes you developed a strong need to withdraw from the world. A natural daydreamer, you have an overactive imagination. Mystical pursuits such as meditation, yoga, and astrology drew your interest. Your life was dedicated to connecting with a higher power. Artistic and creative pursuits were done in hiding. Others might not have realized you had such talents.

Your need for solitude and peace made it difficult for you to spend time with others. Born with empathic abilities, you took on other people's emotions. You lacked boundaries. Sacrificing your own needs led to sadness and depression. At times, you felt lonely, but you preferred your own company. Your heightened sensitivity to energy made being around large groups of people painful.

In past incarnations, you were private, shy, and secretive. There was something about you other people could not figure out. You walked in the spiritual world and were good at escaping from responsibilities. Mundane work and duties stifled your imaginative energy. You preferred solitude to ponder the meaning of life. Being in love and seeking a soul mate were important for your overall happiness. Writing poetry and love songs and detaching from the world around you helped you survive. Suffering and heartache made it difficult for you to find that special someone. You learned in past lifetimes that a higher power was your true parent. People let you down in the past, and it was difficult for you to have a steady routine. Commitment was a struggle because your emotions were unstable. Each day you felt something different and wanted to explore that.

Sleeping brought comfort and your dreamworld was active. Dreaming deeply was a gift and provided precognitive messages that helped you make decisions. You avoided practical responsibilities because they made you feel weighed down. You did not see the importance of holding down a job or committing to things that brought no joy. The real world was a difficult place for you to grasp. Disillusionment and feeling overwhelmed by emotions prevented you from achieving goals.

In previous lifetimes you may have lived in a monastery or hidden away from society in some way. Being a priest, cleric, or rabbi might have been appealing. You spent a lot of time in contemplation. Reading, writing, listening to music, being in nature, expressing creativity, and praying all brought comfort. Helping others was the focus of your life, but sometimes you neglected your own needs. Compassionate and kind, you often felt taken for granted. Sometimes you found yourself in unhealthy relationships because of your idealistic nature. You spent a lot of time trying to figure out what true love was.

At times, you struggled with depression and anxiety. You coped by escaping or using substances like alcohol to numb your pain. You might have had to overcome addiction. The majority of your time was spent seeking answers to life's most complex spiritual topics.

Some tips for keeping the north node in the sixth house and the south node in the twelfth house balanced in harmony and abundance:

- Be responsible and work hard to achieve goals.
- Focus on being practical, realistic, and productive.
- Serve others in practical ways.
- Organize things and plan for the future.
- Avoid escapism and avoiding responsibility.
- Develop a routine and focus on your health.
- Focus on the details and see things clearly.
- Develop realistic expectations.
- Control worries and anxiety.
- Be responsible and of service as the sixth house asks.
- Surrender, relax, and let go as the twelfth house desires.

North Node in the Twelfth House

The north node in the twelfth house encourages you to seek deep connections with others and develop a spiritual path. You were a giver in past lifetimes, but now it's time to focus on your own inner needs. You are often hard on yourself. Focused on helping others, working productively, and efficiently, you do not always take time for fun or relaxation. Perfectionistic tendencies, worry, and anxiety can make it hard for you to embrace change easily. You like to be in control and want to plan each step of the way. You need to build faith and trust in yourself and others in this incarnation. Realize you don't have to be a workaholic or focus on mundane tasks. It's time to withdraw, reflect, and relax. Going with the flow will help you learn how to rest and enjoy the little things in life.

You worked hard in past lifetimes and focused on serving others. Naturally responsible with high standards, you need to be less critical in this life. Focusing on compassion, forgiveness, and unconditional love is the key to enhancing self-love. You need to take care of your own needs and develop a self-care plan. Doing everything for everyone else is not your mission in this lifetime. Make time in your routine for meditation, journaling, listening to music, tapping into your imagination, and finding an inner calm. Your practical, down-to-earth nature can restrict your ability to let go and relax. Balancing a need to work and a desire to withdraw into solitude will help you connect with your soul purpose.

In past incarnations you focused on the material world, doing mundane tasks for others, and organizing things. You made sure there was enough money to buy food, pay bills, and take care of your health care needs. Being super responsible and at times rigid made it hard for you to enjoy your success. You still like order, routine, structure, and are used to controlling your environment, but in this life it's time to let go and trust the universe or a higher power to tend to your needs. Take more risks and be more vulnerable.

It's time to connect with other people on an emotional level and learn that there is more to life than what you do. Overthinking can block your ability to trust yourself. Tap into your own intuition, and listen to your inner voice. Believe in a higher power. Using your imagination and daydreaming will open you up to your creative side. Allow yourself to ponder and study the mysteries of life. Take classes in spiritual topics that interest you such as astrology, energy healing, crystals, and yoga.

Breaking free from real world responsibilities and relaxing will help you grow. Making time for solitude, calming your nerves, and controlling your active mind will bring a deeper connection with yourself and with others. This incarnation calls for you to focus more on your inner world, which allows you to trust the universe to take care of your needs. Inner peace is the key to loving yourself the way you are. Surrender and let go of perfectionism and remember that you are human. Let the weight lift off your shoulders and explore hobbies that bring joy into your life.

The more you focus on discovering the purpose of life and walking a spiritual path, the quicker you will find true happiness. Developing a good sleep regimen and keeping a dream journal can help you open more to your spiritual nature. Pay attention to your dream messages, gut instincts, and universal signs. Listen to your intuition, eliminate worry, and focus on a spiritual path, and all your dreams will come true.

South Node in the Sixth House

You have mastered hard work and devotion to order, structure, and a practical path. Responsible at heart, it's hard for you to have fun. You were always busy doing mundane tasks such as cooking, cleaning, taking care of children, and doing small acts of service. In past lifetimes you focused on duty and paying bills for material survival. Frivolous endeavors did not interest you and caused anxiety. You always felt an inner push to accomplish things. Neglecting your own needs and sacrificing your time for loved ones became your life's purpose.

You had a natural talent in serving others, organizing people's lives, and giving them advice to help them meet their basic needs. Often feeling unfulfilled yourself, at times you sought a deeper emotional connection through your service and work. Focusing on the day-to-day routines, repetitive expectations, and small details led to burnout. Sacrificing your energy and time for others with problems led to compassion fatigue. At times, you valued others more than yourself. You might have believed it was selfish to concentrate on your own self-care. Telling people no and standing up for yourself were difficult life lessons. Sometimes you continued to give your all even when you received little in return.

Committed and dedicated, you developed high standards and expectations of yourself and others. Perfectionism, obsessive-compulsive tendencies, worry, and anxiety plagued your life at times. You found it difficult to shut down your active and complex mind. Trouble falling asleep and staying asleep were common. You often woke up during the night replaying song lyrics or thinking about something at work that you wanted to do or say. You found it challenging to let go, release pent up anxiety, and free yourself from the need to be productive.

In previous lifetimes you probably served in some aspect of the medical field such as nursing, physical therapy, personal training, nutritional care, or helping people who were physically or emotionally ill. Alleviating the suffering of others by providing practical support fulfilled you. You may also carry a love of animals into this current lifetime and can find comfort by having pets.

You developed strict routines, procedures, and plans. Your priority was perfecting your duties whether they were cleaning, writing, teaching, or taking care of animals or people. You held yourself to unreasonable standards and were critical of your own abilities.

Very few could keep up with your energy and efficient style. You found validation through completing large numbers of tasks. This was your forte. You focused on self-improvement, exercise, diet, and taking care of your health. There were lifetimes where you suffered illness and developed a fear of getting sick. These experiences made you more disciplined regarding the care of your physical body.

You pushed yourself too hard and sometimes overworked to the point of exhaustion. Some might have perceived you as a workaholic. It is important to balance the need to achieve and finish things with enough down time to recover from your work.

In past incarnations you found it difficult to balance obsessive thoughts and behaviors. You pushed yourself to the limit and had trouble enjoying life. Relieving stress and controlling your environment came through exercise, diet, organization, cleanliness, and preparation. Control was your way of dealing with change and the unknown. As a master servant, you were always there for people in need.

Some tips for keeping the north node in the twelfth house and the south node in the sixth house balanced in harmony and abundance:

- Balance worry and anxiety.
- Focus on letting go and having fun.
- Learn how to take care of yourself first.
- Develop a self-care plan.
- Remember that no one is perfect.
- Avoid being overly responsible.
- Let go of control and embrace the unknown.
- Focus on a spiritual path.
- Use your imagination and express your creative side.
- Go with the flow.
- Overcome obsessive thoughts and behaviors.
- Focus on your inner needs as the twelfth house guides you.
- Take care of your physical health as the sixth house requires.

Conclusion

The authors of this book, Carmen and Bernie, want to thank you, the reader, for taking the time to explore this material. We wanted to leave you with a positive description of how each pair of the nodes of the Moon encourages soul growth and your search for harmony and love.

Whatever nodes of the Moon you have at birth, you can find the love and creative success you hope for along this life path. It is a fact that past life patterns follow us into our current life, and it is quite possible to turn any issues you have from your past into a winning road to inner strength. There are talents you possessed in previous incarnations that you may discover once again.

If your nodes of the Moon belong to the Aries/Libra or first/seventh house clan, importance is placed on getting to know your true identity. You likely will explore relationships with several different types of individuals. You came here with some fiery Aries restlessness along with the soothing airy mental breezes of Libra. If you happen to have the nodes in a first/seventh house combination, it repeats this emphasis on self-focus in the first house, similar to the sign Aries, and adds a need to balance this approach in relationships through the seventh house, similar to the sign Libra.

You can have the best of both worlds by discovering a deeper part of your inner world and celebrating milestones in the external one. Learning patience helps you achieve your goals and maintain solid relationships. The Aries inner warrior guides you to accept new challenges. The Libra influence reveals a need to keep your life in balance. If you have a first/seventh house pairing, the same can be true in establishing a clear identity and rejoicing in finding close friends and lovers.

These node pairings by either sign or house want you to master facing adversity along with taking the time to pause and take an objective, insightful view. You will thrive when finding your independence and discovering people who support your most cherished dreams.

If your nodes of the Moon belong to the Taurus/Scorpio or second/eighth house tribe, you possess a steady determination to achieve your life goals. Some may accuse you of being stubborn, but you explain this as a need to slowly process important choices. Both Taurus and the second house appreciate comfort and stability while Scorpio and the eighth house will sometimes follow passion into situations that are not for the timid.

You likely don't respond well to being pressured. Learning flexibility keeps your life flowing more smoothly. Finding individuals you can trust in times of happiness or sorrow is highly valued. You came into this incarnation to develop a healthy self-esteem and to find the wisdom to stay clear of those trying to manipulate you. Believing you can turn negative experiences into positive ones — whether from past lives or experiences in this life — empowers you.

On occasion, the universe may pull something away from you that is no longer needed. It could involve a negative thought process or a job or relationship. This node combination tends to resist change. In letting go of something that is keeping you from feeling centered and happy, you may experience a rebirth into a new energy. The main message here is not fearing change.

If your nodes of the Moon belong to the Gemini/Sagittarius or third/ninth house family, you came into this life on a fast track to seek new stimulating mental adventures. You likely get bored easily if you don't have enough challenges in front of you. You are blessed with an ability to guide others through their problem areas. Giving advice *when asked* to do so by the people closest to you wins their appreciation.

This node combination, whether by the signs (Gemini/ Sagittarius) or the houses (third/ninth), urges you to learn focus. Doing so allows you to develop creative power and to follow through on the goals you hope to achieve.

Communication is at your fingertips constantly with this node duo. You can become skillful as a teacher, writer, and consultant. You likely enjoy friends and lovers who express their thoughts openly. Your mind often visualizes ways to stay inspired. Those who negate your dreams simply don't understand the way you operate. The universe spontaneously reveals synchronistic experiences that maintain a youthful movement in your mind and body. When you live your life without worrying about the future, you attract the harmony and abundance awaiting you.

If your nodes of the Moon belong to the Cancer/Capricorn or fourth/tenth house group, you entered this lifetime with a strong intuition. You might not readily reveal your emotions unless you really trust someone. You likely value family and community. The saying "your home is your castle" applies to you. You are not a spontaneous person but would rather mull over your choices until they feel right.

You have an innate drive to find a career that suits your talents. There are times when getting away from a stressful job or other responsibilities rejuvenates your spirit. You treasure your comfort zones. There is nothing wrong with this. When you embrace a new experience that goes beyond your usual routine, it can stimulate new insights.

You tend to remember positive and negative experiences from the past in this life.

Focusing more on what you can control brings greater happiness. You brought great inner strength earned from past incarnations into this life. This carries you through any adversity you encounter. Believing in your ability takes you to the top of the mountain of success.

When you commit to friendships or romantic relationships, you prefer loyal individuals. You care deeply for those you love and need this in return. If there are scars from past relationships, a new soulmate can make past pain disappear.

It must be said you have a tendency to cherish your privacy. Not everyone will understand this about you. People giving you enough space to be yourself gains your admiration.

If your nodes of the Moon belong either to the signs Leo/Aquarius or the fifth/eleventh house affiliation, you were born with tremendous willpower—whether you consider yourself an introvert or extrovert. A steadiness and reliability colors your mental approach to life. As a result, others tend to lean on you for advice and support. Sharing center stage with those you love brings them closer. Both the signs and the houses in this group grant you creative insights. Your independent streak could lead you to be a trendsetter in following your most passionate goals.

Learning to pause to gain objectivity about situations makes for clearer decision-making. Being patient with lovers and friends allows your relationships to flow in greater harmony. Appreciating what you have already achieved in terms of work and love makes for inner peace and joy.

Past life patterns have less of a hold on you when you avoid power struggles. This does not mean it is wrong to fight for your most heartfelt beliefs. Working toward win-win solutions with others resolves a crisis or tension faster.

You enjoy having a friend who is also a lover. Having friends and a lover to celebrate with makes you feel on top of the world. Learning from the past and embracing the present with confidence paint the future with a broad brush of adventure as well as stimulating energy.

If your nodes of the Moon belong either to the signs Virgo/Pisces or to the sixth/twelfth houses, you entered this life with wonderful healing energy and a drive to excel at whatever work you choose. Karmic patterns have less of a pull on you when you follow the paths of your highest beliefs. Knowing when to stop trying to be too perfect allows your mind, body, and spirit to feel at ease with a sense of oneness.

These are the signs and houses that could find you in service or healing work. You probably have a keen eye for detail. Becoming well known for developing a skill is within your mental reach.

You likely don't like criticism by people on a regular basis. The stronger your faith in yourself the less impact the opinions of others stop you from finding happiness and success. You have a longing to find a soul mate with similar beliefs or at least someone able to accept your own ideals.

In relationships, partnerships, and friendships, honoring your own needs proves more beneficial than choosing to ignore them. It's also vital to pay heed to your inner awareness about the people in your life. Don't deny what you truly perceive in someone just to stay with that person.

Pacing yourself is essential to your physical and mental health. Meditation, walks in nature, taking quiet moments to recharge your energy, listening to music, or anything that enables you to escape stress are good for your soul. You may have a strong attraction to oceans or other bodies of water as a way to self-heal.

You possess a powerful intuition. When you trust this inner dimension of yourself, the universe has no choice but to deliver happiness, love, and fulfillment of your most cherished dreams.

From the Author's

Thank you for purchasing *Astrology's Magical Nodes of the Moon*. Our sincere wish is that you enjoyed the book and found insights and tips that you can implement in practical ways in your life. If you have a few moments, please feel free to add your review of the book on the online site you purchased from. We would appreciate your feedback. If you would like to connect with us you can find our website links below.

Carmen Turner Schott, MSW, LISW

Carmen is a practicing clinical social worker and astrologer with national and international clientele. She started studying astrology after an experience with a glowing ball of light in her doorway when she was in high school. She has been working with children, adults, and trauma survivors for over twenty-five years. She is also the founder of Deep Soul Divers Astrology. Visit her at www.CarmenTurnerSchott.com.

Bernie Ashman

Bernie is an internationally known astrologer. He is the author of several astrology books that have been translated into other languages. He enjoys serving his many clients. Bernie first discovered astrology in 1973 and has lectured throughout the United States. Contact Bernie at www.BernieAshman.com.

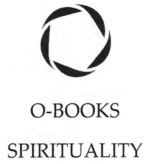

O-BOOKS

SPIRITUALITY

O is a symbol of the world, of oneness and unity; this eye
represents knowledge and insight. We publish titles on general
spirituality and living a spiritual life. We aim to inform and
help you on your own journey in this life.
If you have enjoyed this book, why not tell other readers
by posting a review on your preferred book site?

Recent bestsellers from O-Books are:

Heart of Tantric Sex
Diana Richardson
Revealing Eastern secrets of deep love and intimacy
to Western couples.
Paperback: 978-1-90381-637-0 ebook: 978-1-84694-637-0

Crystal Prescriptions
The A-Z guide to over 1,200 symptoms and their healing crystals
Judy Hall
The first in the popular series of eight books, this handy little
guide is packed as tight as a pill bottle with crystal remedies
for ailments.
Paperback: 978-1-90504-740-6 ebook: 978-1-84694-629-5

Shine On
David Ditchfield and J S Jones
What if the aftereffects of a near-death experience were undeniable? What if a person could suddenly produce high-quality paintings of the afterlife, or if they acquired the ability to compose classical symphonies? Meet: David Ditchfield.
Paperback: 978-1-78904-365-5 ebook: 978-1-78904-366-2

The Way of Reiki
The Inner Teachings of Mikao Usui
Frans Stiene
The roadmap for deepening your understanding of the system of Reiki and rediscovering your True Self.
Paperback: 978-1-78535-665-0 ebook: 978-1-78535-744-2

You Are Not Your Thoughts.
Frances Trussell
The journey to a mindful way of being, for those who want to truly know the power of mindfulness.
Paperback: 978-1-78535-816-6 ebook: 978-1-78535-817-3

The Mysteries of the Twelfth Astrological House
Fallen Angels
Carmen Turner-Schott, MSW, LISW
Everyone wants to know more about the most misunderstood house in astrology — the twelfth astrological house.
Paperback: 978-1-78099-343-0 ebook: 978-1-78099-344-7

WhatsApps from Heaven
Louise Hamlin
An account of a bereavement and the extraordinary
signs — including WhatsApps — that a retired
law lecturer received from her deceased husband.
Paperback: 978-1-78904-947-3 ebook: 978-1-78904-948-0

The Holistic Guide to Your Health
& Wellbeing Today
Oliver Rolfe
A holistic guide to improving your complete health,
both inside and out.
Paperback: 978-1-78535-392-5 ebook: 978-1-78535-393-2

Cool Sex
Diana Richardson and Wendy Doeleman
For deeply satisfying sex, the real secret is to reduce the heat,
to cool down. Discover the empowerment and fulfilment
of sex with loving mindfulness.
Paperback: 978-1-78904-351-8 ebook: 978-1-78904-352-5

Creating Real Happiness A to Z
Stephani Grace
Creating Real Happiness A to Z will help you understand
the truth that you are not your ego
(conditioned self).
Paperback: 978-1-78904-951-0 ebook: 978-1-78904-952-7

A Colourful Dose of Optimism
Jules Standish
It's time for us to look on the bright side, by boosting
our mood and lifting our spirit, both in our interiors,
as well as in our closet.
Paperback: 978-1-78904-927-5 ebook: 978-1-78904-928-2

Readers of ebooks can buy or view any of these bestsellers by
clicking on the live link in the title. Most titles are published
in paperback and as an ebook. Paperbacks are available in
traditional bookshops. Both print and ebook formats are
available online.

Find more titles and sign up to our readers' newsletter at
www.o-books.com

Follow O books on Facebook at **O-books**

For video content, author interviews and more, please subscribe to our YouTube channel:

O-BOOKS Presents

Follow us on social media for book news, promotions and more:

Facebook: O-Books

Instagram: @o_books_mbs

Twitter: @obooks

Tik Tok: @ObooksMBS

www.o-books.com